I went there on my bike

The University Years

Jim Mackley

By the same Author

A Child in Paradise?: Wymeswold 1939–1958

Adventures of a Civil Servant

Copyright © 2021 Jim Mackley

New edition © 2025

All rights reserved.

ISBN-13: 9781917130233

*For Peter and Jon, who indulged me when I said:
"I went there on my bike!"*

CONTENTS

I bought a bike	1
I applied to go to University	2
I went to University	5
Life at University	8
The University	14
Manchester	18
France 1	22
Summer in Wymeswold	30
Back to Manchester	33
I went to Besançon on my bike	35
Besançon	42
Biarritz	55
September 1960	60
Pontarlier	63
Antibes	85
Back to Pontarlier	87
Belley	94
Plouha	101
Manchester 3	104
Getting a job	120
The Final Fling	127
Epilogue	130
Appendix: Saint-Exupéry and the Meaning of Human Existence	139
Acknowledgements	192

I bought a bike

Soon after my thirteenth birthday, I got a job as a paper boy in my native village of Wymeswold in Leicestershire. I was paid twelve shillings a week (60 pence). I worked for about three quarters of an hour in the morning and half an hour in the evening, six days a week. I saved most of the money and the following year I bought a new bike. A *Raleigh* would have cost over £15. My Uncle George was a blacksmith and had dealings with a firm called Pells of Peterborough, who made bikes. He managed to get me a bike called a *Pello* at trade price for just over £13. It was basically a *Hercules* bike with *Pello* stamped on it. It was a solid "sit up and beg" touring bike.

I applied to go to University

If it had been suggested to me at the age of 14 that I would have to go to university, I would have been horrified. I was a shy little boy (hardly big enough to carry the newspaper bag) and I had hardly been out of the area between Loughborough and Nottingham, apart from two trips a year to see my grandparents in Skegness. The thought of living away from home did not appeal to me in the slightest. Only two boys from the village had ever been to University and I didn't find out about one of them until sixty years later!

I was at Loughborough Grammar School. The expectation there was that most boys in the 'A' stream, where I was, would go to University. It was no big deal, there: that was what people did. So I drifted into the sixth form. After that, the only questions were: can you get into Oxford? If not, which lesser university can you get into?

In late 1957 I spent a couple of interesting days at Oxford, mixing with posh boys from Winchester and other public schools and having interviews at New College and Worcester College. I remember one of the janitors saying to a colleague how young I looked. This was true anyway, but the whole intake was two years younger than had been the tradition. Unlike most other universities, Oxford and Cambridge had insisted that male students did their National Service before they went to University. However, those, like me, who were born after 30th September 1939 were no longer required to do National Service. (I was born 34 days after that date!) The consequence was that there were two or three times more candidates for Oxford and Cambridge at that time. I didn't get in!

Lawrence Jackson was vicar of Wymeswold at that time. My father was his churchwarden. Trinity College, Cambridge, owned most of the land in the village and were patrons of the church. Lawrence suggested to me that he might be able to get me into Trinity College, if I wanted to study theology. I declined – I was terrified at the thought of standing up in front of the congregation twice a week delivering a sermon. (My father told me many years later that Lawrence had expressed relief that I didn't get into Oxford, presumably because he thought I would be out of my depth socially.)

There was no university clearing system in those days. So, we had to apply to each university individually. We were advised to apply to seven. Colin Tivey, the head of French at Loughborough, called a meeting of the six or seven of us, who were thinking of reading French. He said that King's College, London, and Manchester were the best places for French. Perry and Stevenson should put down King's College as their first choice and Mackley and Murray should put down Manchester. I wasn't at all unhappy about that because my father had a cousin who lived in Manchester and I had been to stay with them when I was sixteen. I think Perry did go to King's. Stevenson went to Leeds and Mackley and Murray went to Manchester.

I don't remember all the universities I applied to, but I do remember that I applied to Manchester, King's, Leeds, Newcastle and Hull. I had an interview at King's, but wasn't offered a place. I told myself that they were miffed because I had chosen Manchester above them. I also had an interview at Leeds with a German professor or lecturer. I had applied to read Modern Languages (French and German) there. They said they would accept me for French, but not German. In February 1958, I sat an examination (at school) for a Scholarship at Manchester University. I was offered a place at Manchester in the School of French Studies, without interview. So, the first time I set foot in Manchester University was when I arrived as a Fresher in the autumn of 1958.

I went to University

On the basis of my 'A' Level results, Leicestershire County Council gave me a County Bursary of £240 a year. I applied to get into a Hall of Residence, but was unsuccessful. The University found me digs at 20, Salisbury Road, Chorlton-cum-Hardy, just round the corner (about half a mile) from where my father's cousin lived – Uncle Willie, Aunt Alice and their sixteen year-old daughter, Ann. In those days most students lived in digs in their first year. That is: they lived with a couple who provided bed, breakfast and evening meal and full board at the weekend. In our case the couple were Mr and Mrs Higgins.

20 (left) and 22 Salisbury Road. (2020)

I shared a room with Derek Wood from Burslem, Stoke-on-Trent, and a lad called Brian from Middlesbrough. Derek was a great extrovert with a strong Potteries accent. He was reading Architecture. Brian was one of the most introverted people I ever came across, though, once he had got to know us, he was quite argumentative. He was reading Maths. Two Laotian students shared another room, while an "older" (30 year-old)

Indonesian, called Santosa Sumadibrata, had a single room to himself. The top floor of this Victorian house had been converted into a flat, which was occupied by three second and third year students. Before we had been anywhere near the University, Derek, Brian and I had paid our shillings to become Life Members of Chorlton-cum-Hardy Billiards and Snooker Club!

Me, Santosa, medical student, Derek and Brian, top floor, 20 Salisbury Avenue, 1958

All the first year students were invited to a Freshers' weekend. I remember a few things. We went to a Church service at Manchester Cathedral. Sitting not far from me was a young man with a very big birthmark on his face. I remember feeling very sorry for him. His name was Bob Davies and he became a good friend of mine – he came to our wedding six and a half years later. Of course, after the initial shock, one didn't think about the birthmark and it certainly didn't seem to affect him.

The Freshers also went to the Sports Centre, where we were lectured on the need to keep active, even though, as we were no longer at school, physical education was no longer compulsory. We were also encouraged to join clubs and reminded that we were no longer at school and were now responsible for organising our studies.

Life at University

I was enrolled in a BA French Honours course. The Head of the School of French was Professor Eugène Vinaver, a very distinguished academic, who specialised in the 17th century dramatist, Racine, and Old French (11th to 15th centuries). There was also another professor, Professor Lloyd Austin. Other senior lecturers included Dr F.E. Sutcliffe, Dr Gilbert Gadoffre and Dr Frederick Whitehead. Both the first two were made professors before I left.

All first year modules were compulsory. On the literature side we studied only two authors: La Fontaine (*Fables*) and Flaubert (*Madame Bovary* and *Trois Contes*). Professor Austin ran this course throughout the year.

Dr Sutcliffe was a Yorkshireman who rattled out his lectures in a rapid monotone. In the final year, he lectured us on the philosophers Montaigne, Descartes and Pascal.

I didn't have that much to do with Dr Gadoffre, but he twice had an important influence on me. In one seminar he told us how to write an essay. First write down everything you can think of; then make a plan and slot your thoughts into the appropriate place in the plan. If it was a French *dissertation* the plan had to include an introduction, itself containing three or four elements, a main body divided into thesis and antithesis and a conclusion answering the questions posed in the introduction.

One afternoon, Dr Gadoffre held an extra-mural seminar on the French economy. Since the war, France had appeared to me, as a teenage outsider, to be a poor country with a chaotic Government and a new Prime Minister every other week.

Dr Gadoffre pointed out that, in spite of the political turmoil at the top, the French economy was in good shape. There was a national plan, run by a team of elite civil servants, which provided a sound strategic framework for economic activity. In particular, they had decided to exploit the recently discovered natural gas resources in order to develop their infrastructure.

Dr Whitehead was a Reader in linguistics. For the first few weeks of the first year, he lectured us on Syntax and Semantics. In my immaturity, I skipped some of these lectures, because they were boring. I discovered nearly four years later that there was a paper in the Final Examinations, based on this course. Dr Whitehead was a very shy man, but I remember one of his lectures. He explained the difference between *denotations* and *connotations* – the former provide a neutral designation for an object while connotations carry emotive baggage, for example a person could be called a *man* (denotation) or a *bloke* with its connotations. He divided connotations into *purr* words and *snarl* words.

Other lecturers included Frank Saunders, Mr Daniels and Miss Morgan. There were also some native French-speaking lecturers. Their lecturing style was a complete contrast to the English speakers. Whereas, Dr Sutcliffe was down-to-earth, Jean Gaudon was highly intellectual and 'airy-fairy'. You could reproduce Dr Sutcliffe's lectures virtually word-for-word in an essay, whereas I didn't have a clue what to make of the French lectures – very beautiful, but completely useless.

We also had a series of lectures on mediaeval French. These began with learning the basics of Old French grammar. (This proved unexpectedly useful decades later when my son's doctoral research included literary texts in Anglo-Norman.)

Then we read *La Chastelaine de Vergi*, an elegant thirteenth-century tragic romance.

In those days there was hardly any emphasis on spoken French. The ability to translate to and from French were, however, essential skills. Miss Morgan led the language translation seminars.

There were 70 students in our year. General lectures were held in large amphitheatres. A printed sheet was passed round for students to sign to testify to their attendance. It became apparent very quickly that the system was far from perfect: it was easy to get one of your friends to sign in for you. Indeed there was one chap who only went to one or two lectures in the whole of the three years – he spent most of his County Major Scholarship (the best scholarship available) on beer.

Students who were not doing Honours degrees studied four subjects in the first year, three in the second and two in the final year. For an Honours degree, we had to follow a "General" course for two years in a subject other than French. I chose German. It was also compulsory to have reached the required standard in Latin.

I was very good at Latin, but didn't get a very good mark in 'A' Levels. For reasons that I have found hard to explain ever since, I did three years in the Sixth Form at Grammar School. After two years I got adequate 'A' Levels in French, Latin and German. A year later, I took the same subjects again. The second time round, I got a much better mark in French, the same (low) pass mark in German, but dropped from 55% to 45% in Latin. I thought there were two possible reasons for this. We had a very demanding Latin teacher. He was called "Tocker" Allen. He earned this nickname, because he arrived at the school some 30 years after the English master, who was called "Ticker" Allen – presumably because he was so boring. Anyway, Tocker made us do fiendish translations from English into Latin and I was pretty good at them. So, I was hoping that the 'A' level translation paper would be very difficult. In fact it was very easy; consequently I didn't have chance to shine and so, presumably, got similar marks to everyone else. The more likely explanation for my poorer performance was the following. The 'A' level course contained a strong literature component. Even for someone who is good at Latin, it's not easy to sit down and read Virgil's *Aeneid* in an evening, or even one book of it. That is even more true of Ovid's *Metamorphoses* and Lucretius' *De rerum Natura*, both of which are difficult. By February 1958, I was already assured of my place at Manchester and a grant from Leicestershire County Council, based on my 'A' levels, so I suspect I didn't work as hard as I could have on the Latin literature. The result was that I was obliged to take the Intermediate Level Latin course for the first year. This was an undemanding course, which I completed without difficulty. Indeed I realised at the time that that was the only realistic chance I had of getting a "First" at University. However, I decided to concentrate on getting through into the second year of my French Honours course.

The German course was equally undemanding, but had a considerable bonus. The tutor was a beautiful sophisticated young woman. Completely unattainable, of course, but very good to look at. At school we had all been called by our surnames, but now at University this beautiful young woman addressed me as "Mr Mackley".

I also enrolled for an Intermediate Russian course. I went for about six weeks, learning the alphabet (which I can still work out) and also to write in Russian (which is now still completely indecipherable). I did all the written homework, but decided not to spend time learning vocabulary. This proved to be my downfall, because the lecturer humiliated me when I didn't know a simple word, that she thought I should have known, so I didn't go again.

Derek Wood, my housemate, told us right at the beginning that there were about 42 students taken into the School of Architecture each year, but only about seven graduated at the end of the course. I thought this policy was appalling. Then, in my second year at Mrs Higgins' I was joined by a number of Chemical Engineering students from the Faculty of Technology (recently incorporated into the University, later separated to become UMIST and now, since 2004, part of Manchester University). The Faculty of Technology's policy at the time was similar to that of the School of Architecture: there was a high wastage rate at the end of the first and second years.

The School of French had a much better system. They told us right at the beginning that they believed that they had a good selection policy. They only admitted students, who they thought were capable of completing the course. There was an examination at the end of the first year, but everyone was expected to pass. If anyone didn't get through, the School was to blame for admitting them in the first place. The result was that, out of 72 students in the first year, 69 or 70 went on to the second and third years. Those who didn't negotiated places on other courses.

After that there was only one short examination before Finals. There was a course in the second year on French History, with an examination at the end of it in March 1960. That counted towards the final degree mark. Otherwise the final degree papers were based on the whole of the second and third year courses. More of that later.

Of course, there was much more to University than attending lectures and writing essays. There was a whole new world to discover, both within the University and the city of Manchester. Manchester was rather bigger than my village of Wymeswold (population 770).

The University

The original Victoria University of Manchester consisted of a rather daunting old Victorian building, which housed a museum. I hardly ever went there.

Main University Building c.1950

The School of French was in the Faculty of Arts. The Faculty occupied a sizeable area alongside the main building. The main "Arts Building" was a large neoclassical construction with some large amphitheatres, smaller rooms for seminars and rooms for the more senior members of staff, big enough for tutorials of six or eight. The School of French had its own student common room. All our tuition took place in this building.

The Arts Building

At the end of the plot of land, furthest away from the main road, stood the Arts Library. This was a huge three or four storey building. It had at least one open seating area. Its main feature for me was the stacks: several floors with rows and rows of books. There were individual seats with tables by the windows. That was where I wrote most of my essays. I can still smell the rather fusty atmosphere in those stacks.

The University was situated in one of the poorer districts of Manchester, of which there were many at that time. The outlook from the stacks was rather depressing. Behind the Library was a row of back-to-back nineteenth century workmen's houses. Each had a small backyard with a washhouse, a coalhouse and an outside lavatory. I never saw a human being in any of these houses, but one of them had a dog, which seemed to bark most of the time.

The other important building was the Student Union. This was a recently constructed building and was a good amenity. It had bars, a coffee shop, a modern hall for open lectures, debates, plays and Saturday evening ballroom dancing. In the basement there were table tennis tables and snooker tables. On the top floor there was a sizeable silent room for study.

I went to a number of general lectures there. I remember two of them. One was given by a young and up-and-coming politician, called Roy Jenkins. The other lecturer was a Roman Catholic talking about contraception.

There were regular debates. One which I remember was on the motion "This house prefers Saturday night to Sunday morning". That, perhaps more than anything else I have to say, captures the spirit of the time. It was based on the 1959 film, *Saturday Night and Sunday Morning*. It reflects the young persons' rebellion against the conformist, church-going and prudish society that most of us had been brought up in.

Every Saturday evening there was a big dance in the Students' Union – or rather three dances. This was the late fifties. Discos had not yet been invented, while Night Clubs were outside my budget. The main dance took place in the spacious main hall of the Students' Union building. There was a large live orchestra with one or more vocalists. As had been the case in the Leicestershire villages, Wymeswold and Seagrave, where I had been going before I went to Manchester, most of the dances were so-called "modern" dances: quickstep, foxtrot and modern waltzes. There were the occasional Olde Tyme dances: Gay Gordons, St Bernard's Waltz, Valeta and Military Two-step. There were two other smaller dance-rooms. Both had live musicians. One concentrated on jazz and Latin American music, while the other played the new Rock'n'Roll.

I also joined the Scottish Country Dancing Society, which met once a week in the Sports Centre. They were a friendly group of about a dozen students, mostly Scottish, but not in any way exclusive of Sassenachs. I learned the basic steps and a number of dances. It also enabled me to widen my circle of acquaintances. Early in the summer term the group hired a coach to go to a ball at Glasgow University. We left one Friday evening and travelled overnight. On the coach they taught me to play brag. They were playing for money. I cottoned on quickly and came out with winnings.

This was the first time I had been to Scotland. Indeed, it was the first time I had been north of Blackpool. It was midmorning on the Saturday, when the coach drove us down Sauchiehall Street in Glasgow. I was shocked. The scene was like something out of a Dickens novel, though the trams were anachronistic. The trams went down the middle of the road. There were poor-looking people everywhere scurrying across the traffic to and from the trams.

On the Saturday afternoon, I went to a football match. Queen's Park had just been relegated to the Scottish Second Division, but they played, in front of a small crowd, in the vast Hampden Park Stadium with a capacity of well over 100,000.

I had one item of Scottish attire in my wardrobe: a Royal Stuart tartan tie which an aunt had given me as a birthday present. I borrowed a kilt to wear at the ball. I hadn't been there very long before someone pointed out to me, not too kindly, that my tie and kilt did not match! and that I had no right whatsoever to wear a Royal Stuart tartan.

I spent many hours playing table tennis, which I was good at, and some hours playing snooker, which I wasn't good at.

As I was in digs for the first two years, I went back there most evenings for dinner. I did most of my private studying in the library.

Manchester

It was wonderful to live in a great city like Manchester. Where do I start?

My great passion at the time was football, so I will begin with that. Manchester had two First Division football teams. Manchester United won most of their games, Manchester City didn't. I went to both grounds on a number of occasions. They could not have been more different. It was, of course in the days before all-seater stadia and indeed crowd segregation. A visit to Old Trafford (Manchester United's ground) was an electrifying and somewhat terrifying experience. The land area of the stadium is (or was then) relatively small. This meant that the sides of the spectator terraces were quite steep. The supporters were very partisan and very vocal. The effect was like being in a cauldron with 60,000 other people. Getting out of the ground after a match was a struggle. The exit from the terraces was narrow. Once you had fought your way out you arrived into a confined area between the stand and the outer wall. Through the gate you arrived in a narrow track. After that, in my case, the only way to "freedom" was over a narrow bridge along with 10,000 other people.

Manchester United played in blood red shirts. Manchester City played in wishy-washy pale blue. Their home was at Maine Road. It was built on a vast plot of land and had a capacity of nearly 85,000. But, whereas Old Trafford was like a cauldron, Maine Road was like a saucer. Some 30,000 spectators (I'm guessing) would be spread thinly across the terraces. In general, at that time, the supporters were not so partisan. On the few times I went there, I had the impression that the supporters quickly started criticising the player, if things weren't going well.

I did not, in fact, have all that much time to go to professional football matches. While I was at school, I learned that my friend, John Elsom, had trained to be a football referee.[1] I decided that I would like to be a referee. In the summer before I went to Manchester I wrote to the secretary of the Football Association to enquire how to go about it. I was thrilled to receive a personal letter from the Secretary, Sir Stanley Rous, who was the "god" of the football world at that time. He wrote that he had forwarded my name to the Manchester and District Football Association and told me how to contact them. I went along for some tests (which did NOT include an eye test, which I might well have failed!). I was assigned to referee junior matches in a South Manchester league. (I may have been a shy country bumpkin, but it took some courage (or foolhardiness) to step into that minefield.)

So I bought the kit and most Saturday afternoons I went off on my bike in search of football pitches in the depths of Wythenshawe and Northfield. Wythenshawe, in particular, was a relatively new council development. Most of the players came from pretty rough backgrounds. I survived for one and a half seasons, then went off to France. When I came back, I didn't think about taking it up again, though I did referee one or two University games. The boys came from better backgrounds, but were no better behaved!

Manchester had a large number of cinemas, theatres, restaurants, dance halls and the Hallé orchestra. I went to a dance hall in the city centre only once or twice. The one time I remember I went with the Laotian boys. One of them asked me

---

[1] John had left school at 16 to train as an accountant. I made contact with him some 40 years later, when he was Chairman of Leicester City Football Club. He invited me to a match and I sat in the Directors' box.

to ask a particular girl to dance. I did and she accepted. When I got back to my seat, the boy told me that he had asked the same girl and she had refused – he assumed because he was Asian.

We went to the theatre two or three times a year. Early on in my stay in Manchester, the Laotian boys said that a new musical was coming to Manchester, just before it went to London. They arranged for me to go with them to see it. The musical was called *West Side Story*.

I also went a few times to the Hallé orchestra. The first time I went was to Haydn's *Creation*. I can still see the vast array of musicians, playing together with mechanical precision. I also remember studying one of the violinists for a long time. Eventually, I realised that he worked in the Midland Bank, which I was using at the time. Some years later, I went to the ballet to see *Sleeping Beauty*. At the time, I thought ballet was the perfect art form.

Before I went to live in Manchester, I hardly ever went to the cinema. This was a good period for film going. The Asian boys thought for a long time that the Gaumont cinema was called *South Pacific*, because the film had such a long run there. That was followed by *The Nun's Story*, starring Audrey Hepburn. There was also a cinema in Market Street called the Cinephone. That showed mainly foreign films. I remember going to see *Hiroshima, Mon Amour* and *Déjeuner sur l'Herbe* (based on the painting by Manet) both of which made a big impression on me in very different ways. Later on, there were the so-called *kitchen-sink* films like *Saturday Night and Sunday Morning*, *A Room at the Top* and *A Taste of Honey*, which were very relevant in the changing cultural climate of the time.

Quite early on in our stay, Santosa, the Indonesian, invited Derek, Brian and me to a Chinese restaurant. None of us had ever been to such an exotic place to eat! That was about to change, as there were a number of Indian restaurants within walking distance of the University. Of course, we ate most of our two-course midday meals in the University Refectory – how old-fashioned that sounds now!

For most of the University year it was cold and dark. In the spring of 1959, Brian and I took Santosa to a local beauty spot – Mere in Cheshire. I had just bought my first camera. It was a beautiful spring day. We went into an open grassland area and Santosa – who was quite a stocky man – was gambolling around like a spring lamb. Suddenly, he saw a clump of lush greenery and dived into it. "Jim, what is it? What is it?" he yelped! He had just thrown himself into a bed of nettles: he had never seen nettles before. Later in the summer, Santosa came to stay with me for a few days at my home in Wymeswold. I lost touch with him soon after that, but I have often wondered what happened to him. Nothing good, I suspect: soon after that Indonesia got entangled in a series of bloody civil wars, some of which targeted so-called intellectuals.

Coming from a village, it seemed natural to me to get involved in local activities. Accordingly, I went to the local church. I joined a badminton club in the Methodist Church Hall. I also went to Stretford Church and joined their bell-ringing team. In Wymeswold I had been a keen bell-ringer. We had six bells and, mainly at my instigation, had learned to ring a number of peals for five or six bells. At Stretford they had eight. I learned a whole new lot of peals. On one occasion I biked to Knutsford for a bell-ringers' meeting.

France 1

While I lived at home, I was never particularly interested in going to France, because it would interfere with playing cricket. However, I hardly played any cricket in Manchester, so that argument no longer applied.

In the summer term of 1959, my friend, Bryn James, told me about a scheme for going to France for a month or so to work in a children's holiday camp, looking after French children, all expenses paid, plus pocket money. Accordingly, I wrote to the Central Bureau for Educational Visits and Exchanges in London. That letter changed my life!

On the afternoon of 18th June 1959, I arrived at the railway station at Dole in the Jura Department of France. Dole was on the old RN5, which ran from Paris to Geneva, 222 kilometres from the latter. I had been told that someone would meet me at 18:00 hours. As I was early and hot and thirsty, I wandered round the town looking for something to drink. I remember having a beer and feeling even more thirsty. I went back to the station, but all was quiet. I was beginning to get a little apprehensive.

Suddenly, a gaggle, a cacophony, of excited French girls appeared apparently from nowhere. I got on a coach with them and we were taken to the *Château de Crissey*. This was in fact an old manor house, set in its own grounds, which had been converted into a youth hostel. It was very comfortable and well-appointed. (I discovered later that this was a rarity among French youth hostels: most of them were scruffy and not at all welcoming.)

We were all going on a 10-day training course for would-be *moniteurs* or *directeurs* in *colonies de vacances*. In fact, most of the girls had no intention of working in a *colonie de vacances*: they had just completed their teacher training course and were obliged to follow this extra course as part of the training.

On arrival, I was directed to a dormitory, which I was to share with four other males. Three of them were head teachers in primary schools, who were going to be *directeurs*. They were older men in their thirties, while I was still only nineteen. Charles Baudard and Maurice Moyse lived in Besançon, while André Proudhon lived out in the sticks in the Doubs Department. The other male was a chap about my age, called François, who was also going to be a *moniteur*. We got on well together. I kept in touch with Charles until he died prematurely many years ago. I also went to see André Proudhon in his village, Arc-sous-Cicon, a year or two later – he took me into the forest looking for a special type of mushroom – *morilles*.

André, Charles, me, François and Maurice

Soon after our arrival, we went to the dining room for the evening meal. The course members had been divided into teams. Each team had one male and five or six females. Each team had a separate table. I was with Colette, Josette, Michèle, Paulette and Danièle. The first four had just finished teacher training. Danièle had just completed her first year at University and like François and me, was actually going to work in a *colonie de vacances*. I never saw Colette again. I went on my bike to see Josette a couple of times, when I was in Besançon and, likewise, Michèle, when I was in Pontarlier. Michèle was a butcher's daughter, so I expect I had a good meal, when I went to see her. Danièle Borgazzi lived in Pontarlier, so I saw her the following month. She invited me for Christmas lunch with the family on Christmas Day, 1960. We had snails and I had to fight with her brother to get my share. She came over to stay at our house in Wymeswold during the Christmas holidays of 1961, much to the chagrin of my then girl-friend, Margaret. I lost contact with Danièle after that.

After all these years, Paulette is still a good friend. But, it is pure chance that we have remained in contact. She came to see me in Pontarlier with her fiancé, Jean, in 1961. After that we lost contact until 1979. Then Paulette was sorting through her papers and found my 1959 address. She wrote to me. My parents had left that address in 1969, but, as we had lived in a small village, the postman had been a friend of my parents and knew their new address. He forwarded Paulette's letter to them and they forwarded it to me. We called to see them that summer on the way back from holiday in the south of France and have stayed with them many times since. Their daughter, Elise, also came to stay with us in England in the late eighties.

Josette, Danièle, Elizabeth, me, Colette and X
(Elizabeth and X were English girls)

I thought I was in paradise at Crissey. There I was in the company of five girls, who, presumably because I was "different", found me interesting. The weather was perfect. Everything was new: the food, the language – the girls didn't have quite the same vocabulary as Racine or Flaubert – the culture. We were shown all sorts of ways of keeping the children interested. In particular, we learned a lot of French songs, most of which I can still remember. Looking back, I suppose that was the time that I fell in love with France.

> *Adieu donc m'amie je m'en vas, adieu donc m'amie je m'en vas,*
> *Puisque mon bâtiment s'en va, puisque mon bâtiment s'en va,*
> *Je m'en vas faire un tour dans Nantes*
> *Puisque le roi me le demande.*

Puisque dans Nantes tu t'en vas, puisque dans Nantes tu t'en vas
Un corselet m'apporteras, un corselet m'apporteras
Un corselet avec des manches,
Brodées de soie rose et blanche.
Mais quand dans Nantes fut arrivé,
Mais quand dans Nantes fut arrivé,
Au corselet n'a plus pensé, au corselet n'a plus pensé
N'a plus pensé qu'à la ribote
Au cabaret avec les autres.
Mon Dieu, qu'est-ce que m'amie dira ? Qu'est-ce que m'amie dira ?
Tu lui diras, tu mentiras, tu lui diras, tu mentiras,
Tu lui diras que dans tout Nantes
Y'a pas de corselet comme elle demande.
J'aimerais la mer sans poisson, j'aimerais la mer sans poisson,
Et la montagne sans vallons, et la montagne sans vallons,
Et le printemps sans violettes
Que de mentir à ma Jeannette !

After Crissey, I was invited to spend the weekend with a family in Dole. This was the first French town I had visited outside Paris. Like many French towns, it had many old stone buildings. It had a large basilica, which I was told was a cathedral. I found it strange that a town smaller than Loughborough, where I went to school, should have a cathedral. It was also the birthplace of Louis Pasteur.

My host owned a *quincaillerie* – an ironmonger's and hardware store. He appeared to be very well off. He owned a Citroën DS – the 'bees' knees' of French cars in 1959. He had a son who was about my age. One day he drove me with two or three of his friends to Dijon. The objective was to show off his driving 'skills'. We reached 150 km per hour on the RN5! The son also said something to me which I have always remembered. He was showing me the bathroom. The washbasin (or toilet) had a sort of fancy plug or flush. He said: *c'est typiquement français : c'est très beau, mais ça ne marche pas.* It's typically French: it's very beautiful, but it doesn't work!

Early in the following week, I was driven through miles and miles of forest up to the village of *Les Grangettes*, the most beautiful place I had ever seen. I had been allocated to work as a *moniteur* in the *Colonie de Vacances de la Croix-Rouge de Dole* there. There was a *Directeur*, Henri Roux, and eight *moniteurs*. All the children were boys from the Dole area, aged from about five to fourteen. I had a team of ten-year olds. The reality was much different from the theory taught at Crissey! The main concerns were not how to teach them to sing songs – though we did that as well – but to get them to do what we wanted them to do, to try to prevent them from hurting themselves, to get them to eat food that they didn't want; and to go to sleep when they didn't want to, especially in the afternoon for *la sieste*. I also had to learn a whole new vocabulary, not to be found in the works of Racine: socks, vests, underpants, dustbins etc. I also learned that *je ne sais pas* was pronounced *shay-po*.

I said that *Les Grangettes* was beautiful. It was also very primitive. It had a Spanish-style church, built when the Franche-Comté was ruled by the Spanish, with a discordant church bell. This competed for attention with the cow-bells attached to most of the cows in the surrounding fields. Each farmhouse had a dung-heap at the side of the road. Some of the roads were tarmacked, but many weren't. The location was fantastic. The *colonie de vacances* building was purpose-built and therefore only used for two months in the year. There was accommodation for about 80 children in dormitories. The staff shared small dormitories. It had been built on a hillside about 500 metres from the *Lac St-Point*, the third largest lake in France.

Lac St-Point

The lake was about 850 metres above sea-level. Situated in the Jura mountains, it was surrounded by pasture land and pine forests. As it was sunny for most of the month of July, while I was there, the lake was always blue. There was an impressive medieval castle – the *Château de Joux* – just beyond the northern end of the lake.

While I was there, I spent a lot of my time with the other *moniteurs*. Some afternoons, presumably during the siesta, we wandered down to a bar in the next village, *Oye-et-Pallet*. We also managed to borrow a small rowing boat which we could take on the lake. On my first day-off I walked round the lake with a chap called Michel. It was about 21 kilometres. It was the first time I had ever spent so long out in the hot sun.

Chateau de Joux (2020)

Consequently, my legs got sun-burnt, but no lasting damage was done – on the contrary, my legs tanned easily after that. On other occasions a chap called Jean-Michel lent me his *mobylette*, a motorised cycle. At that time one didn't need a licence to ride them in France. I went into Pontarlier and a ride round the mountains. I also went to a village called *Les Verrières* one afternoon. The village straddles the Franco-Swiss border. I walked into Switzerland and back again to get my passport stamped – four times!

The last night at *Les Grangettes* there was a fantastic thunderstorm. Looking out of the window, I could see the lake lighting up over and over again. The next day I travelled back to Dole to catch the train home. I remember waiting at the station for the train. It was a hot day. My suitcase was overflowing, with the sleeping-bag strapped outside. I was wearing a thick high-necked pullover and a jacket, because they wouldn't fit in the suitcase.

Summer in Wymeswold

It was not only in France that 1959 was a good summer. It was also the best summer in England since 1947. For some years, I had had a holiday job working in a grocer's shop in the village of Sileby, seven miles from my native village. I went there on my bike nearly every day. (On odd occasions, when the weather was bad, I got a bus to Loughborough and then a train to Sileby.) The shop was a big old-fashioned grocer's shop. Coincidentally, the owner's son, Ronnie Hill, had been in the same class as me at school, but this was more of an embarrassment than an advantage – I was his dad's employee. The main shop was in Loughborough – the biggest and best grocers' in the town. There were four other employees in the Sileby shop. The manager, Eric, who was married, but not averse to extra-marital relationships, Fred, Peter and Charlie, who were all single – and very different. Fred, like Eric, was middle-aged (which, I suppose, when you are 19, means 'over thirty'!). He 'fancied' one of the customers. Peter was about 25 and also fancied one of the customers. Peter, like me, was a good table-tennis player and we found somewhere to play sometimes. Fred, Peter and I often played dominoes at lunch time. Charlie was homosexual, though at that time, talking about that was taboo. He frequently asked me to go 'up the apples' with him to the storeroom, but I managed to avoid being there alone with him.

I enjoyed working in the grocer's shop. In the course of the years, I did all the jobs in the shop, apart from boning bacon. One of my first jobs was to skin a Cheddar cheese. This was a horrible job. The cheese was big, heavy, greasy and smelly. It was hard work for a small sixteen-year-old. My main job was making up orders. Customers phoned in their orders to Eric or Fred. We put the goods into cardboard boxes and Charlie delivered them. Quite a lot of food still came in bulk – lard, cheese, biscuits – and we had to weigh them and put them in paper bags or grease-proof paper – hardly any plastic in those days! We were allowed to eat the broken biscuits, which meant that sometimes more biscuits were broken than should have been. I knew the price of everything in the shop. Apart from butter and eggs, the prices didn't change very much from year to year. I can still remember that a tall tin of Heinz baked beans was 1/4d, while a small one was 8d. A bottle of whisky was an enormous 37 shillings – over a third of a working man's weekly wage! They paid me £5 a week for four full days and two half days.

I also served in the shop and was quite good at working the cheese cutter and ham slicer. Towards the end of my career in the shop, I was briefly allowed to use the bacon slicer. That indulgence came to a bitter end, after I cut my finger. A week later one of the customers came back to the shop with my blood-stained bandage, which she had found in her bacon!

In that summer of 1959, my parents had been married for 23 years. They had never spent a night in a hotel together. They decided to go on a week's coach holiday to North Wales. (My father had never been 'abroad' before.) They had a wonderful time and glorious weather. (They repeated the experience the following two years – to the Isle of Wight and Great Yarmouth with diminishing returns.) At this time my 79-year old grandmother had had a house built just down the road from my parents. She was charged with looking after me, while my parents were away. As, by this time, I had developed a taste for

Indian food, she decided to make me a curry – a complete novelty for her. I think she was quite excited about doing this and she spent all day preparing the meal. But she was deflated afterwards: she told my mother "He gobbled it up in three minutes!"

Back to Manchester

Having passed the preliminary examination in June, I returned to Manchester in October 1959 to embark on a two-year course leading up to finals at the end of the third-year. This would be interrupted by a compulsory term in a French University and a voluntary year working in a French school. Nevertheless, the work that we did (or didn't do) in October 1959 would be examined in June 1962. I will return to the main coursework later in the run-up to finals.

There was one two-term course with an examination at the end of it, which counted towards the final degree. This was a French history course, focused on the eighteenth century. We had a good lecturer, Dr Hampson, and we learned about the works of Montesquieu and tried to understand the French Revolution. In spite of my best endeavours, I did not do terribly well in the examination, scoring a Lower Second Class.

We also had a twelve-week course of lectures from a visiting professor, Professor Wagner, on *phrases hypothétiques*. Twelve hours on 'if' clauses! He was a good lecturer. As a consequence, I know much more than most French people about the construction of 'if' clauses and rarely make a mistake!

I stayed in the same digs in Chorlton-cum-Hardy, along with Brian. All the others changed. Most of the newcomers were studying Chemical Engineering at the Faculty of Technology. They were a boisterous crowd. One evening when we came back to the digs "someone" had hung a red light stolen from some road works outside the front door of 20 Salisbury Road. Mrs Higgins was furious and gave us all notice to leave. The others all left, but eventually Brian and I were allowed to stay as we had been "led astray".

Brian hardly ever went out other than to go to the University for his lectures. He was, however, a member of the Mathematics Society. At Christmas in the first year, he decided, uncharacteristically, to go to their Christmas Party. As he was very "tight" with his money, he decided to go on his bike, as he did every other time he went to the University buildings. He had a smart newish "racing" bike with drop handlebars. The next day he was very crest-fallen: his beautiful bike had been stolen. By the following Christmas, he had acquired an old bike. He again decided to go to the Maths Christmas Party on his bike. That bike was stolen too!

I went to Besançon on my bike

After two terms at Manchester, we had to spend the third term at a French University of our choice. Montpellier and Grenoble were the favourites. I chose to go to Besançon, partly because I liked the area and partly because I hoped to meet Josette, whom I had met at Crissey, again. Besançon proved quite popular with my fellow students, because it had the best language laboratory in France. So there were five or six of us who went there from Manchester, including my friend Bryn James. Bryn and I decided to try to get a flat together, which we did.

I decided that it was pointless spending a lot of money on train and boat fares to get to Besançon. I was going to go on my bike. So, I put my bike on the train from Chorlton-cum-Hardy to Loughborough and proceeded to prepare myself to cycle the 500 miles from Wymeswold to Besançon. My parents were quite worried about this, especially as my bike was quite old and bulky. My dad offered to buy me a new bike, but I declined. I was not sure that a so-called touring bike would be any better. In particular, all the advice was to have a small hard saddle, whereas I had a soft wide saddle. I read a book and did take advice on another matter: this was to build up gradually to a cycling tour. So, in the ten days before I left, I built up from five miles a day to 45 miles. Thus I was able to bore my children afterwards by saying "I went there (i.e. anywhere within a 20 mile radius of Wymeswold!) on my bike."

I joined the International Youth Hostels Association and planned my route so that I could spend as many nights as possible in youth hostels. (Other than Crissey, which I discovered was not at all typical, I had never been near a Youth

Hostel.) I decided I wanted to take my tennis racket. So I bought an attachment and fastened the tennis racket to the front wheel. I already had a decent saddlebag, but I bought a pair of panniers to attach to both sides of the back wheel. I had battery-powered front and rear lights and my faithful Hercules 3-speed gears. I was very careful to ensure that I didn't get my clothes wet. I had a cape and hood and persuaded my mother to make me a waterproof covering for my shoes. I would wear shorts so that my trousers would not get wet.

On Sunday morning the ninth of April 1960, I set out from Wymeswold for Market Harborough and on to Greens Norton in Northamptonshire, where I spent the night in the Youth Hostel, as planned. So far so good! The next two days did not go according to plan. I had hoped to take minor roads as far as possible, but my next planned stop was in central London. So, for much of the Monday I had to ride along Watling Street (the A41), which got increasingly busy the nearer I got to London.

I reached the Youth Hostel in London in late afternoon. There were a large number of young people with suitcases milling around and it was fully booked. I was told that there was no point in trying the other London youth hostels, as they would be full as well. So I set off for Cudham in Kent. Until then I had thought that Kent was a flat county, but the Youth Hostel, which I reached late in the evening was on the top of a hill. Instead of the planned 50 miles a day, I had cycled about 90 miles that day.

On the Tuesday, there was a ferry from Folkestone at about 4 o'clock in the afternoon. I set out in the morning, but I was determined not to spend the day riding along the main roads. So I bought a local map and sketched out a route across country. Unfortunately, this meant that I had to stop at every road junction to decide which way to go. The result was that I missed the ferry at Folkestone and had to cycle over the Downs to Dover Youth Hostel. It was a wet and windy evening and there is a big hill between Folkestone and Dover.

I went down to the port on the Wednesday and bought a ticket for me and my bike on the ferry to Calais. My bike was attached to a winch and was carried through the air on to the boat. I arrived in Calais. Almost immediately I came upon a large French square. In those days, the norm in France was for traffic from the right to have priority. So the drivers came into this square from all directions, knowing whom they had to give way to and whom they didn't. I had no idea, but somehow, I managed to get to the other side. With hindsight, I was quite lucky to survive. It was only some weeks, months or years later, that I learned that the rule in France, unless there is a sign to the contrary, is that any traffic coming from even a minor road or a field on the right has priority. In those days there were hardly any 'give-way' or 'stop' signs.

It was just as windy in northern France as it had been in Dover. Having got out of Calais, I rode along the road to St. Omer. The land there is flat. The wind was blowing from the west. With my tennis racket and panniers attached to my bike I was leaning into the wind. When I went past a house at the side of the road, I was suddenly sheltered from the wind and I fell off my bike. The inhabitants of the house all came to their window to laugh at me! I got back on my bike and found my way through St. Omer to the youth hostel at Arques. The youth hostel was attached to a café. I remember I had egg and chips. I think I was the only guest that night. The following morning, I had breakfast in the café. There were working men in the café drinking their glass (or two) of red wine for breakfast. In those days there were warning posters in cafés and other public places, urging people to limit themselves to a litre of wine a day!

The previous year I had ridden a moped in France. I had decided that the trick for riding on the right side of the road was to start off on the correct side. After that there would be no problem. However, the youth hostel was at the end of a track. When I got to the end of it, I set off on the left-hand side, but fortunately realised my mistake before too long. There was a more or less direct route from Calais to Besançon, but again I decided to take the byways. I bought a map for 1.10 New Francs (just under 10 pence) and I set off eastwards. I discovered that the towns and villages in that part of France have Dutch-sounding names of which the first was Hazebrouck. I also discovered that most of the roads were still cobbled. A French friend told me later that there is a cycle race (or part of a race) which is referred to as *l'enfer du Nord*. A feature of the map was that it showed a lot of broken bridges – bridges which had been destroyed during the war, but which had not yet been repaired when the map had been printed. At the time, I found that strange as it was *fifteen* years since the end of the war – three-quarters of my lifetime. With hindsight, I realise that it was *only* fifteen years since the end of the war! As I cycled through the flat countryside, I rode through village after village. Each village had its church, its *mairie*, its post office, its café and a number of farm-houses, each with its *fumier* (manure heap) alongside it. I was surprised to see that in some of the fields the ploughs were still drawn by oxen.

I had lunch in a place called Estaires. Each day for lunch, I either bought some ham and a *baguette* or went to a restaurant. The standard price for a three or four course meal was 5 or 6

New Francs (about 50p). A cup of coffee was 50 new centimes. Earlier that year de Gaulle had created the new franc. One New Franc was worth 100 old francs. However, until the introduction of the euro 42 years later, most people of my generation or older still counted in old francs. So *mille balles* meant 10 New Francs! In the course of my journey, I soon learned that French restaurants opened at 12 noon and closed at 2 o'clock. So there was no point in turning up at a quarter to two and expecting to be fed.

One of the real bonuses of cycling in France was the milestones (or more correctly kilometre stones!) There was one every kilometre on the side of the road. They had red tops on National roads and yellow tops on Departmental roads. They showed the distance to the next town and the distance to the next village. In addition, there was a smaller white stone, numbered 1 to 9, every 100 metres. So it was easy to break down the journey into manageable chunks.

I spent the next night in a youth hostel in either Douai or Cambrai. I had heard that French youth hostels were grotty, but to date that had not been my experience. That was about to change, so it is perhaps as well that I can't remember now where I stayed or whether I stayed in both of them on successive nights. Nor do I remember much about it other than that it was … grotty!

During my training period in Wymeswold, I had developed a rash on my (bare) legs. I went to see Dr Robinson, who said he thought it was an allergic reaction to some tinned salmon I had eaten. By the time I got to a place called Bohain, the rash had got worse and so I decided to go to a doctor. He said that it was probably an allergic reaction to the wind or exercise. He gave me some cream and advised me to rest. That would have been a bit difficult, given that I still had another two or three hundred kilometres to go. The doctor did not charge me for the consultation.

My journey took me next through the small town of Guise. On the way there, my three-speed cable broke. I found a small garage in Guise and the owner said he could repair it for me. But it was almost mid-day and, like everyone else in rural France at that time, he was closing for lunch and would be back at 2 o'clock. The cable was quickly repaired and I set off again towards Laon. A few kilometres south of Guise, for the one and only time on the journey, I felt like giving up. I got off my bike and tried to thumb a lift with a small pick-up truck that was passing. Fortunately, the driver didn't stop and so I was obliged to soldier on.

I approached Laon late on Good Friday afternoon. I was impressed! I had been cycling for two and a half days through flat, fairly uninteresting countryside. Then it appeared before me like a medieval citadel on a hill-top, bathed in evening sunlight. I fell in love with the place. I have visited it two or three times since. On the last occasion, we visited the cathedral, immediately after looking round Reims cathedral. I found Laon more impressive – more restrained and a better atmosphere. There is a shroud there with a face imprinted on it, which claims to be the face of Jesus, which I found deeply moving.

When I arrived in Laon, all the bakers' shops had signs outside saying *plus de pain*, which I discovered meant *no* more bread! There was no youth hostel in Laon, so for the first time on my journey I had to look for a hotel room. I found one without too much difficulty.

The scenery changed after Laon. The next day I rode in undulating countryside through the vineyards of Champagne. I spent the night in another hotel in Epernay, which is at the heart of the champagne-producing territory. On Easter Sunday morning, I was riding past the impressive *Champagne Mercier* building. I decided to stop and indulge myself in a conducted tour.

The roads were busy that day and there were no obvious ways of avoiding the main roads. So I cycled on to Vitry-le-François and joined the main road from Paris to Strasbourg, which was even busier. Nevertheless, I managed the 29 kilometres to St Dizier without incident. I spent the night in the youth hostel there.

The following day, Easter Monday, it rained most of the day. The terrain was almost mountainous, as I rode through forests. I experienced for the first time the low clouds in the forests. Surprisingly enough, when I drive through similar forests, fond memories of this day flood back. Again I decided to abandon the main roads and made my way to Nogent, where I spent the night in a hotel.

It had stopped raining, when I set out on the Tuesday morning. I had a clear idea of the route, but was not sure how many of the 130 kilometres I could do in one day. My first goal was Langres. The *Plateau de Langres* marks the watershed between the Mediterranean and the English Channel. The source of the Seine is there.

Besançon

I carried on. By this time the adrenalin was flowing and I soon found myself at Gray, about 50 kilometres from my destination. Later that afternoon I rode through the gates of 25 avenue Carnot, Besançon. I was greeted by the owner, a doctor's wife (or widow, I don't ever remember meeting her husband). She was a distinguished-looking woman, probably in her fifties. She showed me to the apartment on the first floor. She said that she had thought that Bryn and I were a mixed couple. The apartment only had a double bed. It was, however, a well-furnished apartment with polished wooden floors. She only showed mild embarrassment about two chaps sharing a bed. Such was our innocence that I did not think there was anything strange about it either. We certainly did not think of taking part in any – what would have been then – illegal activities.

Me in the kitchen at 25 avenue Carnot

I had sent my trunk by train from home to Besançon. The apartment was just down the hill from the main station, but I received a notification that my trunk had been delivered to a small station on the other side of the city. I went there and discovered that there was a customs post there and I had to declare the belongings, which I wished to import.

I had also arranged for my maintenance grant to be sent to the Besançon branch of the *Crédit Lyonnais* bank. However, when I went to the bank, my money had not arrived. I persuaded Bryn to lend me some money, which he did with understandable reluctance. On one of my visits to the bank I discovered that it closed between mid-day and 2:00 p.m. It was possibly the same day that I discovered that all the shops closed for the same length of time, with the result that the centre of Besançon was completely deserted during this period.

Besançon is a beautiful city. It is surrounded by forested hills. The river Doubs meanders through the city in a horse-shoe shape. The "open" end of the horse-shoe is closed by a hill with a citadel on top built by Vauban. I had not heard of Vauban before I went to Besançon, but I have seen plenty of his work since. Indeed, I can see his *Fort Carré* out of the window now, as I type this in Antibes! Vauban was Louis XIV's military architect, who built strongholds all round the edge of seventeenth century France. (At that time Antibes was on the border of the independent *Comté de Nice*.)

La Citadelle de Besançon

Besançon is a very old city. It was called Vesontio by the Romans. There are several Roman constructions in the city, including a triumphal arch, *La Porte Noire*, in the centre. It was from the 10th to 17th centuries that it was most important; during that period it was the seat of an archbishop in the *Franche-Comté* of Burgundy, which in turn was part of (or under the tutelage of) the Holy Roman Empire and Spain. Consequently, the vast majority of the buildings in the centre of the city were more than 300 years old.

The purpose of the term in Besançon was supposed to be to go to the University. We duly enrolled and were given a programme of lectures. Attendance was voluntary and the lectures did not sound very interesting. We went to a few. We also met our fellow students. They were mostly American, but there were also a Swedish and Danish girl. They also knew a girl called Floriane and we went to her house one day. Floriane spoke about a girl from Britanny, Denise Tessier, with whom I was to work later in the summer. Small world! There were no native French speakers on the course! We also had access to the language laboratory, which had been the main attraction for most of my colleagues from Manchester. Again, I went once or twice, but it was disappointing. We did, however, have access to the canteen in the *Cité Universitaire*. This meant that, for a modest sum, we could have one or two square meals each day. I quite liked the food. Or maybe I pretended to, because I was at the stage where everything French was good. Some of my English friends, Roy Reader in particular, said the food was disgusting, picking insects out of the lettuce to prove his point.

The weather was hot or seemed to be most of the time. The walk from our apartment to the *Cité Universitaire* took me through part of the medieval city, along the banks of the Doubs and over a large number of drains. These were very smelly.

La Boucle du Doubs, Besançon

There is a large *brasserie*, the *Brasserie Granvelle*, at the bottom of the *avenue Carnot*. There were few televisions in France at that time, but they had one. I remember standing at the back of the room, watching the European Cup Final. Real Madrid beat Eintracht Frankfurt by seven goals to three!

I went on some long bike rides to Baume-les-Dames and beyond. The countryside was unbelievably beautiful. One day the owner of our apartment invited Bryn and me to her country house on the banks of the River Ognon, a few kilometres from Besançon. This was a wonderful day. In the morning, Bryn and I swam in the river. That was the first time – and possibly the last – that I had ever swum in a river. Afterwards we had a simple lunch. I do not normally like spinach, but we were served spinach with cream, which was delicious.

One day I was in the *Cité Universitaire* with a fellow student, who was from Southampton University and whom I did not know all that well. I bumped into Jean-Michel, with whom I had worked when I was at Les Grangettes the previous year. Thinking that we were close friends, he invited us both to stay with him one week-end at his home in Pont-de-Roide, which is near Montbéliard in the north-east of the *département*. We duly went and Jean-Michel met us at the station. We were just coming out of the station when we met an old man coming towards us. *Voici le paternel,* said Jean-Michel, as he proudly introduced us to his father. He was a retired railway worker. They appeared not to have much money, but for the Sunday lunch, the father produced a bottle of good Burgundy wine. We were all horrified, when my fellow guest reached over to the jug of water to pour some water into his wine. In his defence, it was quite normal at that time – maybe it still is – to mix wine and water.

Fortunately I was able to stop him in time and explain that it was not the done thing to pour water into *good* wine.

Bryn and I decided to experiment with hitch-hiking. We formed the opinion fairly quickly that it was not a good idea for two young men to stand side-by-side on the road trying to hitch a lift. So we took it in turns for one of us to try to thumb a lift, while the other hid somewhere. When a driver stopped, we asked politely if he could take our friend and they usually did. For our first outing we headed for Germany. Although we had both studied German for seven or eight years, it was the first time either of us had actually been to Germany. First of all we had to negotiate the customs at the border at Breisach. Then we headed for Freiburg, which is a beautiful old city on the edge of the Black Forest. There we stayed at the Youth Hostel, which was just under a kilometre from the centre of the city. The youth hostel was quite modern and certainly of a much higher standard than any that I had stayed in recently in France. My German proved to be totally inadequate. I went into a shop to buy four eggs – supermarkets were rare in those days, one had to go to the counter and ask! I got to the counter and I could no longer remember the German for "four" or the German for "eggs". On the Saturday morning, I wanted to walk into the city centre. As I approached, there were a number of signs with arrows indicating *Einbahnstrasse*. As there were so many signs pointing to that street, I thought it must be one of the main streets and so I decided to follow the signs. It was quite some time before I realised that I was getting nowhere and that *Einbahnstrasse* is the German for "One-way-street".

Hitchhiking in Switzerland

Our next excursion was to Switzerland. We went due east from Besançon to Neuchatel and Bern. Bern was a sleepy old city. I remember seeing a statue of the black bear, which is the emblem of the city. On the Saturday morning we made our way to Basel. I was struck by how Germanic the city was: no-one spoke French and their Swiss-German was incomprehensible. We made our way back into France and stopped at a café. It was the day of the English FA Cup Final and Wolves were playing Blackburn Rovers. The match was being shown live on the television in the café. The commentary was in German. Bryn was not very keen, but I insisted on staying to watch it. Hitherto we had had no problems getting lifts and it was "only" 65 kilometres from Basel to Belfort, where there was a youth hostel. It must have been about 6:00 p.m. when we set off. What I had not realised was that it was much easier to get a lift in the daytime than on a Saturday evening. We walked a long way. After an hour or two a farmer picked us up and took us a little way and eventually we arrived in Altkirch. Still 34 kilometres to go! The map that I am looking at now shows that the road is edged with green, meaning that it is a "pleasant itinerary". That is not my recollection! We walked most of those 34 kilometres.

When we eventually arrived at Belfort, tired and with very sore feet, it was long past the youth hostel closing time. We decided to go to the railway station. It had a large hall with a tiled floor and a bar along one side. We decided to camp down on the floor against the wall nearest to the railway line. It was the first time I had lain down on a stone floor. I discovered quickly how uncomfortable it was. After an hour or so I had a sore back as well as sore feet. After some time we moved to the opposite wall nearest to the road and the entrance, but it was no more comfortable. There were some rough-looking older men at the bar. They tried to draw us into a conversation. In particular they said that if we went with them they would give us a comfortable bed to sleep on. I was not very streetwise at that time, but I did have the sense to realise that that would probably not be a good idea. As the night wore on, they became more insistent and, we sensed, more threatening. At about six o'clock, we decided we had had enough and made a run for it. The men followed us for a short way, but we were young and they did not catch up with us. We got a lift back to Besançon without further incidents.

In spite of this experience we were not put off. Neither of us had been much further south than where we were. Both of us were attracted to the idea of seeing the Mediterranean for the first time. We duly set off in early June. We got lifts to Grenoble on the first day and spent the night at the youth hostel there. The youth hostel was situated the other side of a level-crossing with a flimsy barrier. I was somewhat shocked to see a number of pedestrians scurrying across the railway line, after the barrier had come down.

We set out in the morning to try to get a lift along the *Route Napoléon* to the coast. This was the road through the mountains that Napoleon had taken 145 years earlier to return to Paris after escaping from Elba. We spent the whole morning at the side of the road without getting a lift. Early in the afternoon, I got a lift in a sports car with a young British army officer, who said his name was Robin. He did not have room to take Bryn as well. So I travelled with him all the way through the *Hautes-Alpes* and *Basses-Alpes*. We went through the towns of Sisteron and Digne, stopping at a café in one of them for an afternoon drink. The mountains got more and more barren, the scenery more and more impressive. It was dusk by the time that we arrived at a place that I had never heard of called Juan-les-Pins. Robin said he had a small tent and asked if I wanted to share it with him. Again I showed my naivety, because I did not hesitate to accept. I am pleased to say that my confidence in him was completely justified and nothing untoward happened. The following morning he demonstrated his officer qualities by giving me tasks to perform before breakfast.

We then went down to the beach together. I lay on the beach for an hour or two, soaking up my first experience of – and exposure to – southern sun. Bliss!

I had arranged with Bryn that, if we got separated, we would meet at a hostel in Nice. This hostel was not a standard youth hostel – it was slightly superior – but it was listed in the Youth Hostel book. So, round about lunch-time I left the beach reluctantly, and set off to try to get a lift to Nice. I was unable to find anything to eat, other than a kilo of oranges, which I consumed in the course of the afternoon. I eventually got a lift from Antibes to Nice and found my way to the hostel, which was situated in the hills in the north of the city. Bryn also made his way there. In the evening, I was not hungry, but extremely thirsty. (I was probably suffering from sun-stroke.) I asked at the hostel for a drink, but all they could offer me was a litre bottle of milk – which I drank. My mother had told me when I was a little boy that oranges and milk don't mix. I remembered that advice too late. We were allocated beds in a dormitory. I am not sick very often, but in the night I knew I was going to be sick. I put it off for as long as I could. Then I got up and rushed to the toilet door. As soon as I opened the door, I was sick. Except that … the door I had opened did not lead to the toilet, but to a store-cupboard full of clean bed-linen! I was not popular the following morning – to put it mildly.

The next day, we made our way to the Cap d'Antibes. The hostel we stayed in there belonged to the same organisation as the one in Nice. The management had already been informed of my misdemeanour by the time we arrived. However, we strolled around the Cap, taking photos of each other at the gates of expensive properties. There were lots of palm trees: neither of us had ever seen a palm-tree before. So ended my first visit to Antibes. Little did I think that 40 years later it would become a second home for me!

We were separated again on the return journey. I got a lift at Cannes with another Brit in a sports car. This one was going back to London, but dropped me somewhere en route.

Cap d'Antibes, June 1960

The Danish and Swedish girls invited us to spend a *nuit blanche* with them at the Summer Solstice. We went up into the hills somewhere, taking food and drink with us. But my hopes of some sort of high jinks were sadly disappointed. My only recollection is of feeling tired afterwards!

I went to see Charles Baudard one day. I think Maurice Moyse also went. We played *pétanque* together. Charles also took me to a football match. Besançon played in the second division of the French league and were not very good. On the other hand Sochaux, which was just down the road near Montbéliard, had a first division team, financed by Peugeot, who had their headquarters there.

Charles talked about recent French history. He said, in particular that the English – it was always *Les Anglais* never *Les Britanniques* – had bombed the station at Besançon at the end of the war. At the time, as a twenty-year-old, I thought the war was ancient history, but with the benefit of hindsight I can see that for someone fifteen or twenty years older, it was still very much etched in his memory. I was also surprised by the number of French people that I met during my extended stay in France, who spoke in awe of Winston Churchill.

The other Charles – de Gaulle – had come back to power in France the year before. Charles Baudard said to me one day: *De Gaulle n'a jamais oublié Yalta.* It didn't mean anything to me at the time, but that short sentence goes a long way to explaining Franco-British relations between 1959 and 1969. A conference was held at Yalta in the Crimea in February 1945. Stalin, Roosevelt and Churchill were present, but de Gaulle was not invited. The conference decided the post-war organisation of Germany and Europe. Although de Gaulle operated from London during the war, he was often side-lined from strategic discussions. His exclusion from the Yalta Conference added to his resentment. I don't think it is too much of an exaggeration to say that these experiences coloured his attitude when the UK applied to join the European Common Market.

At that time I was not sure about de Gaulle's position on the world stage, but I thought he was good for France. Between 1946 and 1958 France had had a series of weak governments, whose rise and fall were the butt of music-hall jokes. The franc was weak. De Gaulle brought stability to government and introduced the New Franc which stabilised the currency. He came to power to solve the Algerian crisis. But that crisis continued to rage for another four years afterwards. During that time my opinion of de Gaulle changed, but that is another story.

On 14th June 1960, de Gaulle made a television broadcast to the French nation. I watched it on French television in a bar near the *Pont Battant*. He spoke slowly and clearly; he was easy to understand. This was one of a series of broadcasts over the years. His statements were often Delphic and could be interpreted in different ways by different audiences. But the emphasis shifted each time. So, at the beginning he seemed to be in favour of *Algérie française*, while at the end he was in favour of *autodétermination*. The June 1960 broadcast was noteworthy as it was the first time he mentioned *décolonisation*.

Biarritz

As my stay in Besançon came to an end I began to think about the summer. I decided to write to the Central Bureau for Educational Visits and Exchanges in London. They arranged for me to work again as a *moniteur* in a *colonie de vacances,* this time for an organisation called the CCCS (*Centre pour la Coopération Culturelle et Sociale*). Floriane also worked for them. They sent me to work at their *colonie de vacances* at Anglet near Biarritz.

I had originally intended to go on my bike (900 kilometres), but decided against it, because I was feeling a bit under the weather. So I took a series of night trains across the *Massif Central* to Bordeaux and on to Bayonne. This was my first experience of travelling by train at night. It was not a pleasant or restful experience. There were some soldiers on the train across the *Massif Central.* I remember one of them saying *La France est bossue par ici !* France is a bit bumpy round here.

Unlike *Les Grangettes,* Anglet was a mixed *colonie.* The Director was a woman, Huguette, who was a schoolteacher in Colombes, north-west of Paris. Most of the children and staff were housed in a nineteenth century manor-house set in extensive grounds. I slept in a small one-person ridge tent. That was to be my home for the next two months. During those two months, we had a lot of sunshine – and a lot of rain! Most of my things were mouldy at the end of the period.

I arrived before most of the other children and monitors. This proved to be an advantage, because I could answer most of the children's questions about where things were authoritatively. As a consequence, unlike at *Les Grangettes,* I never had any problems with discipline. I was allocated a team of the youngest boys – 5 to 7 years old. This was tedious in some ways – bed-wetting etc. – but there were no problems with discipline and in subsequent years I always chose to look after *les petits*.

The *colonie* was situated about a kilometre from the sea – a long beach on the edge of the Atlantic Ocean. There were big rollers on the sea. When the children were allowed to bathe in the sea, the monitors joined hands in a semi-circle, to keep the children under surveillance. We could see the sea from the upstairs window of the main building. One day I caused some amusement when I said: *On voit la mer d'ici!* Perfectly correct French, but phonetically open to a different interpretation. We walked down to the sea most days.

There were eight monitors and teams of children, four were male and four were female. Then there was the Director, Huguette and her husband, Guy, who looked after the finances. Then there was a nurse. Her husband, Maurice, was a monitor. He was an old man of 31!

On my first day off, I went on a day trip to Spain with a fellow monitor. His name was Jean. He was from St. Brieuc in Brittany. We caught a coach in Biarritz and set off along the coast through St. Jean de Luz, which had been very fashionable in the 19th century, and Hendaye with its extensive flat beach at the foot of the Pyrenees, right on the Spanish border.

I had never been to Spain before – and it would be another 20 years before I went again. Spain, at that time, was very foreign and slightly sinister. Franco had been in charge with his authoritarian regime for over 20 years. The tourist industry was not well developed.

Our coach took us to Pamplona, where we visited the bullring. Then we went to San Sebastian, with its beautiful beach, crowded with Spanish people bathing in the sun. At some point I wrote a postcard to my parents. As I was going to the coach I remembered that I hadn't posted the card. I came across a middle-aged man in a suit and thrust the card into his hand. The card arrived two or three months later! Also at some point we went to a restaurant for a meal. I don't remember the meal, but, whenever I have a glass of cheap Spanish red wine, I remember the slightly harsh taste of that first glass of that beverage. Come to think of it, it was probably more than one glass, because I kept falling asleep on the coach back to Biarritz, banging my head on the "safety" catch on the window, every time I nodded off.

We took the children on excursions. The main one was to La Rhune, a mountain in the Pyrenees on the French and Spanish border. The summit was technically in Spain, though the only access was from France. We went there through Basque towns and villages. One evening we went to see a Basque dance show, which was very picturesque. I won a bottle of cheap sparkling wine, which I declined to drink, as I had already discovered in Besançon that cheap sparkling wine made me ill. (I persisted with that belief for many years, but, since then, either the quality of wine has improved or my tolerance has increased, because I don't have that problem now!) We also went to watch games of *pelote basque*, played against a wall with a *chistera*.

We also went through the *Landes*, miles and miles of flat land with pine forests, to a large lagoon at Hossegor. And we went to Hendaye, where the beach was very flat and much safer for the children to bathe.

I don't remember much about the other monitors. There was a Laotian chap, pronounced *Lang*. He was a bit older than me, both world wise and world weary. He spoke fluent French, but with a strong accent. Everything seemed to amuse him! Denise Tessier came as a *monitrice* at the end of July. There was also a tall, sophisticated girl, called Eliane, who lived near Huguette and Guy. I came across all of these again within the next two or three years. One evening, a group of monitors broke the rules and went out on the tiles to Biarritz.

The CCCS was running three three-week *colonies* at Anglet in that summer of 1960. I had been recruited for the first two. Towards the end of the second one, Huguette asked me if I would stay and work for the third one. I was flattered to be asked and would have liked to, but I had promised my parents that I would go home in September. Eventually I agreed to stay for another 10 days. The third batch of monitors were a rumbustious lot and we had a lot of fun. In particular, we went one evening, with permission this time, to the *Fête de Bayonne*, not quite Rio, but lively, nevertheless. We danced in the streets, singing:

> *Il était une fermière*
> *Qui allait au marché*
> *Elle portait sur sa tête*
> *Trois pommes dans un panier*
> *Les pommes faisaient Rouli Roula*
> *Les pommes faisaient Rouli Roula*
>
> *Stop !*

Trois pas en avant
Trois pas en arrière
Deux pas sur l'côté
Et deux pas d'l'autre côté

It was that evening, that a girl, called Francine, who I thought fancied me (though any attraction was not mutual) used an expression that is common enough, but which I had not heard before. I thought she said: *J'aime bien me marier !* This set alarm bells ringing! What she actually said was: *J'aime bien me marrer !* (I like to have fun!)

September 1960

I spent a night in a room with Francine. I don't quite remember when: it was probably in early September 1960, but it may have been the following year. There were a number of us back in Paris at the end of the *colonie* with nowhere to stay. The young woman who took over as *infirmière* for the second part of the *colonie* had a place in Montrouge. She invited us to spend the night at her place. There was Francine, Lang and a couple of other people. I was both excited and intimidated at the prospect of spending the night in the same room as a young woman. Once again I was disappointed. The floor was very uncomfortable.

I had decided to go home for a few weeks before coming back to France at the end of September. I had heard of a company called *Skyways*, which took passengers by coach and air from Paris to London and back. Accordingly, I went into the *Skyways* office in the *Place de la République* and bought a ticket for 80 New Francs, possibly for the same day. I then got on a coach, also in the *Place de la République,* and was taken to the tiny airport at Beauvais – an airstrip and a shed! We then got on a small Douglas-DC3 aeroplane. It was the first time I had been on an aeroplane and I was more than a little apprehensive. The man sitting next to me tried to reassure me, but spoiled his message by saying that it was only taking off and landing that were dangerous. We flew to Lympne in Kent. From there a coach took us to Victoria Coach Station in London.

I spent three uneventful weeks in Wymeswold. Having spent two months in the sun at Anglet, I was brown all over, apart from the bit covered by my shorts. I remember that the weather in England that September was uninteresting – not much rain, but not much sunshine either – a complete contrast with the South-West of France.

At this point in my story I need to wind back eight or nine months.

At Manchester University, we had an obligation to spend a term in France. We were also given the opportunity of spending the following school year in France. The offer was to work as an *assistant* in a French *lycée*, helping the qualified French teachers to teach English. Among other things, this would mean postponing the final year at Manchester for a year. It seemed to me to be a great opportunity, though I was in a minority: out of 70 of us, only 10 accepted the offer. These included my friends Bob Davies and Godfrey Shaw. Other opportunities for other people arose later on, either immediately after finals, or after completion of the teaching diploma for those who were going to go into teaching. At some stage my friend John Jordan spent a year in France, but I'm not sure when. My friend, Bryn James, did it after he had finished his teaching diploma.

When I put in my application, I was asked where in France I wanted to go. I said the Doubs department. When I left Besançon at the beginning of July, I still didn't know where I was going, so I left my bike and my trunk in Besançon. At some stage during the next three months, I learned that I was going to the *Lycée de Pontarlier*, which is at the very south of the Doubs department. So, on that occasion my wish was granted – not surprising really, because I don't suppose many potential applicants had even heard of it!

I had to go for an interview in London. During an otherwise unmemorable interview, the interviewer advised me not to be too forthright in my advice to fellow teachers, who might not take too kindly to being lectured by what they might consider to be a mere child. I found that a bit odd at the time, as I thought I had long since left childhood behind.

I then went to Paris – via Lympne and Beauvais – for an indoctrination seminar at the Sorbonne. I shared a room with a chap from Bristol, who boasted of his sexual successes with the women of that city. (The exact words he used have been censored.) I also went to see one of the *monitrices* at Anglet, who lived near the Porte d'Italie, and declared my undying love for her. I can't remember her name, but I can still see her beautiful dark brown hair and her beautiful round face. My advances were rebuffed gently but firmly.

Pontarlier

Early in October 1960, I took the train from the *Gare de Lyon* to Pontarlier, along the same track for most of the way as I had taken fifteen months before. The English teacher at the *Lycée de Pontarlier*, Andrée Queney, met me at the station and took me to the school, which was just across the square from the station. Andrée was in her forties. She had fair hair. She was very tiny, well under five feet tall. She had spent a year as an assistant teacher in Edinburgh, so she spoke English with a Franco-Scottish accent.

Her husband, Marcel was also short, but a lot taller than her. He was a little older too. He was a French and Latin teacher at the school. He had been in the French resistance during the war and had been captured by the Germans and escaped several times, only to be recaptured. He had a fund of stories about life in the prison camps. They were set to make armaments for the German army, but sabotaged them by putting in parts that didn't work. He also said that the Germans tried to starve them to death. The only way to combat this was to restrict physical activity to a minimum. One pupil confided to me that Monsieur Queney still did! He was certainly not the most dynamic of teachers. He was, however, a keen handyman. As well as owning their house 100 metres from the school, they had a property in Besançon and two or three old properties in Malbuisson – across the lake from Les Grangettes. Years later, after they had retired, Marcel spent a lot of time renovating the properties in Malbuisson.

They had a son, Jean-François, who was in his first year at the lycée, when I was there.

On that first day, Andrée told me that, not without difficulty, she had found me a room. This was with Monsieur and Madame Robbe-Grillet at 12 rue Querret. It was a quarter of an hour's walk in a straight line from the school – down across the main street, down over the river Doubs and up the hill on the other side. Monsieur Robbe was a retired railwayman, probably an engine driver. Railway workers were well looked after in France, so I imagine he had a reasonable pension. He was a very quiet man, so I don't remember him saying very much. His wife, on the other hand, was one of those people who never stop talking. Added to which she had a rather grating, whining voice. Nevertheless she was very good to me. I had an upstairs room, with a tiny washroom attached to it. There was a stove on the landing outside my room. I don't remember cooking anything, but I do remember boiling my washing and pegging it out to dry in the garden. During the long winter the shirts froze stiff on the line. After a few days, I asked Madame Robbe if she would make breakfast for me. This was an unusual request in France, but after a day's reflection she agreed to do it. They also invited me to play cards with them some evenings, which was again unusual. They had a number of grown-up children, most of whom lived away from home, but their youngest son was about my age and still lived at home.

12 rue Querret, 2012

Lycée de Pontarlier c.1983

I was introduced to the school and a whole new educational system. The first strange thing was that the headmaster, *le proviseur*, was not a teacher, but an administrator. His deputy, the *Surveillant Général*, Monsieur Sapin, was also not a teacher. He was responsible for discipline in the school. There was also an *économe*, a bursar, responsible for financial matters and his assistant, Dorothée. He also had a second assistant, Paule, but I think she arrived later on.

There were several types of pupil in the school. About half were boarders, most of whom stayed at the school for several weeks, before going home for the occasional weekend. Then there were those who came at 8 o'clock in the morning and went home at 6 o'clock in the evening. The others only came to school when they had lessons and were free to leave for lunch or when they had a free period.

There were two corresponding types of *surveillant* or *pion*, as they were more commonly called: those responsible for boarders and those responsible for looking after the day students who weren't free to leave between 8 a.m. and 6 p.m. Together, they were responsible for the "well-being" (*sic*) and discipline of all the students outside the class-room. The teachers' remit began and ended in the class-room. Thus the *pions* were responsible for supervising the dormitories, recreation areas and canteen. They were also responsible for supervising the private study sessions which took place every afternoon. The *pions* were an unruly and rumbustious lot. They certainly didn't lead by example. They were to be my main friends and companions for the next nine months.

Who were they? Most of them were students of one sort or another, trying to earn some money, while pursuing their studies (or not pursuing them, as the case may be!) They were mostly male, which makes me wonder whether there were any female boarders. Many didn't stay for long – I can only think of two that spent the whole year as *pions* – Chapuis and Robardet.

Among the first batch was Gérard Althuser, a young Alsatian. He was very proficient at *Baby-foot*, a game I quickly learned to play at the *Café Français*. I had not been at Pontarlier very long, when he went off to Besançon University to study chemistry – never to be seen again, one might suppose. But no! We exchanged emails earlier this week. Sometime in November 1960, I bumped into him and he invited me to go and stay with his family, who had a farm not far from Mulhouse.

So, one Saturday in December or January, I got on a train or a series of trains, and made my way to his house. That was another new experience! His parents lived in a big old farmhouse, built to withstand the harsh Central European winter. The cows were housed in the cowshed, adjoining the kitchen, thus providing mutual warmth to the animals and humans. It was very cold. On the Sunday they took me to Mulhouse Zoo, where all the pools were frozen solid. I took the night train back to Pontarlier. I don't think I had to change, but I discovered that the train was going to split at some stage and some carriages would go to Pontarlier and some to another town where I didn't want to be! So I had to keep awake to make sure I was in the right section of the train.

I have kept in touch with Gérard for 60 years. In 1969/70 we were both in Africa – he in Cameroon and the Ivory Coast, I in Swaziland. On the first occasion when I took a car to

France in 1973 we went to see him and his wife, Margot, in Montargis. Three years later we went to stay with them in their new house in Gouvieux near Chantilly. We went there several times after that, the last being in 2009.

Another early *pion* was called Zacchini, or similar. He was called up for national army service at the beginning of November 1960. I can still remember his mournful, slightly terrified expression. At that time national service was – or was about to be – for 28 months and would almost certainly include a spell in Algeria. Was he to be one of the 23,196 French soldiers killed in Algeria? I never heard of him again.

A contrasting character was Bordet. He came to the school in December or January. He was the son of a philosophy teacher at Poligny. He had been an officer in the French Foreign Legion. He had been caught in an ambush and shot through the nose. He had been sent back to France to recuperate. He was very sanguine about his experience: "If they'd waited another second, they could have killed me," he said. I never saw Bordet again after I left Pontarlier, but I thought about him, when writing my University thesis on existentialism.

There were a number of strong characters among the *pions*. The strongest was Claude Talon. He was about three years older than me. He came from a relatively poor family in Besançon, where his mother still lived. He had a degree in Natural Science, but had not passed the CAPES (*Certificat d'Aptitude Pédagogique pour l'Education Secondaire*) which all secondary school teachers had to get before they could obtain a permanent teaching post. But Claude was allowed to teach as a replacement for an established teacher who was on sick or maternity leave and that is what he did for most of the year. He still ate most of his meals with the *pions* – and me.

The meals – two of them each day – were probably the high point of the day. I should probably say "the low point". These were the young men who were in charge of discipline in the school. It would be a euphemism to say that their behaviour was "disgusting". We were seated at a long table for about 12 people in a partitioned area at the end of the canteen. The food was fairly good. There was only one plate per person, which was used for the dessert as well as the *hors d'oeuvre* and main course. Red wine was available. It was not very good – Claude said it was doctored with chemicals – but any wine was good for me in those days. But the behaviour! First of all they were very noisy. Secondly the language was uncouth. It was the law of the jungle for the best pieces of meat, with the strongest always winning. Then there was constant bullying of the less strong members of the group. Finally, there was constant sexual harassment of the two young women, Dorothée and Paule, who joined us for most of the meals. Dorothée treated the comments with haughty and amused disdain, but Paule was often reduced to tears.

Claude told me a story about meat one day:

"A Frenchman and an Englishman went into a restaurant one day. They both ordered steak and, in due course, two pieces of steak were placed on a serving dish in the centre of the table: one piece was beautifully succulent and appetising; the other was scraggy and not at all appetising. The Englishman picked up the dish and offered it to the Frenchman. The latter chose the juicy steak and held the dish for the Englishman to take the other one. The Englishman then complained to the Frenchman: 'If you had offered me the choice, I would have taken the scraggy one.' To which the Frenchman replied: 'So you got what you chose, anyway, didn't you?'"

The main object of Claude's bullying was a chap called Chapuis, *ce con de Chapuis*, as Claude invariably called him. Their backgrounds were similar: Chapuis also visited his mother in Besançon; they may well have known each other before they came to Pontarlier. Chapuis was not such a weak character. Perhaps that is why Claude felt the need constantly to put him down, but put him down he did! Every day! Several times a day!

Unlike the *pions*, I was allowed in the staff room. This was a small room, with a lot of books, a bit like the only school library I ever knew, at Loughborough Grammar School, only smaller. I spent quite a lot of time there, but there were not usually more than four or five other teachers there. Most, especially the married ones, came in to school to deliver their courses and then went home again.

There were three grades of teachers. At the top of the pile were the *agrégés*, people who had obtained a higher level teaching qualification. They were paid more and taught fewer hours – 12 hours a week. Next were the holders of the CAPES. Most of the teachers were in this category. They were contracted to work 16, 18 or 20 hours a week – I don't remember which. All these teachers had tenure – once they had been appointed to a post, they could stay there as long as they wished. On the other hand, short of entering the *agrégation* competition, which older people rarely did, there was little or no possibility for promotion: there were no heads of department, and headships were obtainable through a different career path. The third category consisted of auxiliary teachers, people like Claude, who had not yet obtained their CAPES. They did not have the security of a permanent post and weren't paid as much.

Most of the teachers went home for their meals, but four unmarried ones went to a local restaurant, where they had an arrangement for a regular meal at a reduced price. They were Wenger, an Alsatian, Rieu, Louis Garret and a young female Natural Science teacher, whose name I don't remember.

There were three English teachers: Andrée Queney, Louis Garret and Madame Hérard. I didn't have a lot to do with Madame Hérard. She was on maternity leave for most of the time I was there. I think Andrée felt she had a duty to mother me. Louis was struggling to obtain his CAPES at the second or third attempt and invited me into some of his classes to help him. He was a frisky thirty-year old, quite staid in some ways, but childlike in others. While I was there he bought his first car, a Citroën 2cv, which he showed off to me like a girl with a new pony.

As I said earlier, this was a mixed *lycée*. The school years were numbered in the opposite way to the English system. So the pupils started at eleven years old in *sixième* and progressed to *première*, at the end of which they took their first *baccalauréat*. (This first *baccalauréat* was abolished some years later.) The final year did not have a number, but was simply called *Terminale*, or more commonly by the subject group which the student had chosen to follow for the second *baccalauréat*: *Philo*, *MathElem*, or *SciencesNat*. Most of the students wore overalls buttoned down the front all the time they were on the school premises. The boys' overalls were dark grey and made out of a rough material. The girls' were pale pink, blue or green and made of nylon or cotton.

Although the students started to learn English at the age of 11, it was decided that I should take conversation classes only for the three oldest year groups: *seconde*, *première* and *Philo*. Attendance was voluntary. I had twelve hour-long classes a week, four of which were on a Saturday morning – from 8:00 to midday. There were no classes anywhere in France on Thursdays or Sundays. The school was open on Saturday afternoons, but the timetable was arranged so that there were few classes then.

My first class was on Monday 10th October 1960. It snowed that day! The youngest pupils were the most rewarding. They were mostly enthusiastic and keen to learn. The three or four *Philo* students who turned up on a Saturday morning were also friendly and we had a good conversation. On the other hand, there was a class of *première* students on Tuesday afternoons who were particularly obnoxious. They were mostly day students with well-to-do parents. They affected an air of supercilious boredom and superiority, which I found difficult to cope with.

There was a system in French schools that students who didn't achieve the appropriate grade stayed in the same class for the following year. I was just coming up to 21. Some of the *Philo* students were older than me!

After I had been there a few weeks, I thought it might be a good idea to try to learn something in a more structured way. So I enquired if I could join the Philosophy class. My request was granted. So, for the rest of the year I went and sat alongside my students in the Philosophy class, who were preparing for the *Philo baccalauréat*. This was a worthwhile experience. I learned something and I improved my written French by writing all the essays. The teacher was Monsieur Dumont, an older man. He was a devout Catholic and a server in the church. Towards the end of my stay, he invited me round to his house. He offered me absinthe to drink. This drink had been produced in Pontarlier, but had been banned in France since 1915. As far as I can recall, it wasn't a particularly pleasant drink – it was rather bitter. The excitement was in the fact that it was illegal.

Coming from England, where most wine and spirits were prohibitively expensive for an ordinary student, I was surprised how freely available spirits were, particularly distillations of pears, plums and cherries, as well as *marc*, made from distilled grape pulp. Much of this was home made. Claude explained to me once how dangerous it was to make. There was a time in the middle of the process which produced good spirits. At the beginning of the process, the drinks were no good; after a certain point, there was too much alcohol and they became poisonous. I think a licence was required for home distillation, but a lot was produced illegally. It was illegal to "export" these products outside the *département*.

In 1973, we went to stay with my friend Robert (*see* Belley later on) in the Vosges. He gave me a bottle of *pruneau* which his father had made legally, but warned me about the export restrictions. It was very good and so I drank it sparingly. That bottle travelled with me back to Bushey in Hertfordshire, to Brussels, Bushey, Watford and Brussels again before finally being emptied in Skegness in about 2003.

Most of my social life was spent in the company of the *pions*. On the first day that we met, Claude decided that my name would be *Willie*, because all the *assistants* were called Willie. This was because one of my predecessors had been Willie Dickinson. He had been a larger-than-life Irishman with ginger hair and a ginger beard, who had obviously made a strong impression. So *Willie* I became and have remained with three of them for 60 years now!

Le Café Français – still recognisable 60 years later

We spent many hours in the *Café Français*, which was situated in the middle of the main street, near the crossroads on the road between the school and the house where I lived. The waitress, Françoise, was an attractive 25-year old. She was teased unmercifully, but gave back as good as she got with good humour. We spent hours there, but didn't spend very much. Typically we would buy a coffee for 50 old francs and play Babyfoot for hours. Most of the *pions* were very good at it, especially Gérard.

After a few weeks they taught me to play tarot. This is a game, which, at that time, was played mainly in the mountains of Savoy and the Jura. The game belongs to the same family as whist, but is much more complicated. There are 78 cards – four suits of 14 cards each, 21 trump cards and a special wild card. They are the same cards as are used for fortune telling, but we didn't have anything to do with that. We played for money, though the stakes were very small. My "friends" thought they could get some easy money of the English boy, but I learn quickly, when money is involved. I think I made a small profit over the course of the year.

One chap who didn't was a *pion* with the surname of Martin. He consistently lost money. I didn't like him very much, but he persuaded me to lend him about 50 New Francs each month (about an eighth of my salary) so that he could send it to his aged mother. I did that for about six months. To be fair, he always paid me back at the beginning of the next month.

We spent **a lot** of time playing tarot, in the café, in the school and elsewhere. In particular, in February I went to the Mont d'Or skiing with Claude and his girlfriend, Mady. We went out on the slopes, but it had started to rain so we retired to a bar and spent the afternoon, playing tarot. Some four or five years later I taught Jennifer and our friend Bernard to play. We played regularly until we left Walsall at the end of 1966, even buying a new pack of cards. We have hardly played since – but we still have the cards!

Another favourite activity was the Saturday afternoon promenade. Every Saturday afternoon half the population went to the main street and walked up and down the 500 metres between the bridge over the Doubs and the *Porte Saint-Pierre*. The main objective, as far as the young people were concerned, appeared to be to find people of the opposite sex to chat to.

It was all harmless fun ... generally. One Saturday afternoon, however, I was with a *pion* called Gaudet, a young man with strong socialist views. At one point, we decided to cross the road, as one does from time to time. Unfortunately we stepped out in front of a police car whose driver had to brake to avoid us. The two policemen jumped out of the car and asked to see our papers. When one of them saw that I was English he exploded at this foreigner who had come to France and broken their laws. (We had not crossed at a pedestrian crossing.) We were both fined 300 old francs on the spot. I was very upset. I decided that I would not go to the Saturday night dance in the Town Hall, as an act of penance and to save the money that I had spent on the fine. I spent a miserable evening alone in my room instead. News of my criminal activity spread quickly through the school. A few days later, a young woman who worked as a *pion* for day girls told me that her father was a councillor or similar and that if I had asked her she could have got me off. Too late!

The cinema was another entertainment. I found it strange that in France, at least at that time, after dinner one either went home to bed or one went to the cinema. There was a good little cinema in Pontarlier. So sometimes, instead of going home to bed, I would go with friends to the cinema. We would go about nine o'clock, watch some adverts, a trailer or a 'B' film, then go out to the café and return to the cinema to watch the main film which started at about ten o'clock. I remember three of the films that I watched there: *Psycho, La Belle et la Bête* and *Les Quatre Cents Coups*. (I next went to that cinema with Jennifer in 1993, when we saw *Les Visiteurs*.)

In case you have forgotten, the title of this book is: *I went there on my bike*. At some point in October 1960, I went to Besançon to fetch my bike. There was a half-term holiday at the end of October for *La Toussaint*. I decided to go on my bike to Switzerland for a few days, staying in Youth Hostels. On the first day I rode to Lausanne. On the second day, I rode along the lake to Montreux. There I found a café or restaurant, with a beautiful view over the lake and the mountains. I remembered that my grandmother had said that Montreux was the most beautiful place in the world. I was inclined to agree with her. As it was only 15 kilometres or so to my next destination of Château d'Oex, I decided to linger a while. A big mistake!

I rode for a couple of kilometres past the end of the lake, then turned left up a steep mountain. (I have just tried to check the distance on Google, but the road I took appears not to exist anymore!) I pushed my bike for most of the way up the mountain. About a third of the way up, the road forked. There was a bar at the side of the junction. I was very thirsty. The owners spoke Swiss German, which I found almost incomprehensible. I tried to order a shandy and a sandwich. What I got was a large bottle of beer, a large bottle of lemonade, half a loaf of bread and some ham and gherkins. Even in those days, the Swiss franc was quite strong, so my snack cost me the equivalent of seven shillings and sixpence – the price of an expensive three-course meal in a French restaurant. Eventually I got to the top of the mountain. It was nearly dark by then. Nevertheless I careered down the other side of the mountain at great speed, testing my brakes to the full and arrived safely at the Youth Hostel in Chateau d'Oex. I went to a restaurant for a meal and had a good night's sleep.

The following day I rode along the south side of Thunsee to Interlaken. The youth hostel there was quite a way south of the lake and surprisingly primitive. Then I rode on the north side of Thunsee and crossed over to Fribourg. After Fribourg, the route followed an unmade road. I spent the Wednesday night at the youth hostel at Murten on the Murtensee.

That is where I woke up on my 21st birthday! I rode back through Neuchatel, crossed the Jura and rode down into Pontarlier. When I got back to my room there was a parcel from my mother and a lot of cards, some from people that I had not expected to write to me, including one of the girls I knew in Wymeswold, Ann Meadows. I went to the school for my evening meal and was quite excited to tell my friends that it was my 21st birthday. They were not impressed. At that time, at least, the French made more of their 20th birthday. They did, however, condescend to drink the bottle of bubbly that I had bought!

At some point in November or December the snow came in earnest and lasted for about three months. Pontarlier is situated on a plateau some 840 metres above sea-level. When the snow comes everything changes. The river freezes and the roads and pavements are covered with snow and ice. The shops are decorated for Christmas and the whole scene is reminiscent of an old-fashioned Christmas card.

One day in late November, I was invited to stay with a friend who lived in Mouthe. Mouthe is reputed to be the coldest village in France. It lived up to its reputation, that weekend. (Some 30 years later, I took Jennifer to Mouthe in the summer. The temperature was over 30 degrees!)

I went skiing three or four times. The first time Danièle Borgazzi took me. You may recall that I had met her at Crissey in June 1959. She was home from University for Christmas. We went on the slopes on the outskirts of Pontarlier. I spent most of the time trying to get up after falling down. I also went with Mady and Claude to the Mont d'Or two or three times. I got on better with the skiing – I stayed with Mady on the beginners' *pistes* – but had considerable problems with the *tire-fesses* (drag lifts). You are supposed to grab hold of these as they go past and "ski" up the mountain. The opportunities for getting this wrong are boundless! On another occasion I went cross-country skiing with a chap called Bourdon (or similar). He lived in a village to the west of Pontarlier. I enjoyed that, though we probably didn't have the right equipment.

I have vivid memories of Christmas Eve and Christmas Day 1960. Andrée Queney invited me to her house for the *réveillon*.

It was a particularly boring evening. I was left sitting around while she faffed about preparing for the midnight party. They were devout Catholics. So just before 11:30 p.m. we were marched off to the church for the midnight mass. I remember Andrée making a point of telling me that I couldn't take communion, because I wasn't a Catholic. We then repaired back to their house, where we opened presents (there was one for me!) ate cake and drank champagne. Possibly worth the wait, though by this time I was very tired! But the most memorable experience was still to come – the journey home! It was about three o'clock in the morning when I stepped out of their house. It was a beautiful moonlit night – and *minus* 21 degrees! I had never been so cold. And it was going to be over forty years before I experienced such a temperature again – in Sweden in 2003 or 2004.

Danièle invited me to have Christmas lunch with her family. Her father and mother and brother were there. We had snails as a starter. I remember that her brother was quicker than me at eating the snails and so I did not get so many as he did. Danièle's mother, unfortunately, was killed a few years' later, when her car came off the road between Pontarlier and Ornans.

In February 1961, Claude organised a wine-tasting trip to Burgundy. There were four of us: Claude, Mady, Bordet and I. We set out in Claude's Simca car, early on Sunday morning. Our first stop was at a vineyard in Nuits St Georges. There we tasted liberally many different sorts of local wine. The owner offered us 12 bottles of Nuits St. Georges 1959 at something like 1000 old francs a bottle – quite expensive, but that was to become one of the wines of the century!

Our next stop was at a high class restaurant in Dijon, owned by Mady's sister and her husband. We took the most expensive menu – 1700 old francs – more than three times what I normally paid. The meal was very good and suitably accompanied by more good Burgundy wine.

Our next stop was at Poligny, where we called in to see Bordet's father. He was a philosophy teacher at the local *lycée*. There we were offered a glass of *marc*. On the way back to Pontarlier, we went past an English pub. It was decided to stop and buy a glass of English beer in my honour (though I have a feeling it might have been Guinness, that we drank!)

I was dropped off in the centre of Pontarlier. I called in at the *Café Français* and – much to Françoise's amusement – ordered a glass of ... *Vichy fraise* – the mildest possible drink. After all that drinking I did not have a headache the following day. My explanation for that was that everything we had drunk had been of very good quality.

Some five years later, Jennifer and I went to stay with Mady and Claude. They were married by this time and lived in Besançon in a house owned by Mady's parents. One day they took us to Poligny to visit an old friend of Claude's whose father had a wine cellar. We were duly given wine to taste – *Vin du Jura*. Afterwards, the young man asked us to taste something different. He explained that his father had given him permission to clean out an old cellar to convert it into a disco. The cellar had not been used for a number of years and was full of junk. It also contained a full barrel of liquid. He poured a small liqueur glass for each of us. The liquid was clear. It had hardly any taste and certainly didn't burn my throat on the way down. Immediately afterwards, I had this feeling of well-being, as though I had communed with the essence of the grape! The experts had told the young man that the barrel contained *marc* which was a hundred years old.

Long before that, I was invited once or twice to Sunday lunch with Mady's parents at their home in Frasne. Mady's father was a *notaire* and very *bourgeois*, in contrast to most of the people that I came across, who were mostly very down-to-earth. I was, of course, treated very politely and the food and wine were very good.

I had a lot more dealings with another *bourgeois* family. One day, Andrée asked me if I would give private English lessons to a boy in *troisième*. He had had health problems and had fallen behind in English. (I don't think he had very far to fall!) His father owned the pharmacy, right on the cross-roads in the centre of Pontarlier. They were also very posh and a bit more ostentatious than Mady's parents. I was invited for lunch one day and there was an array of glasses, plates and cutlery – in contrast to the school canteen where there was one place setting for all courses.

The boy's name was Gérard. I gave him weekly lessons for several months. Towards the end of my stay, I suggested that we went on a bike ride together. After some hesitation his mother agreed. We set off one Saturday morning and spent the first night at Neuchatel in Switzerland. The next day, we cycled along the *Bielersee* to Biel. We cycled to the railway station, put our bikes on the train and travelled back to Pontarlier.

I used to like to go to Switzerland. It was still a little exotic. Every time I went I had my passport stamped four times – by the French and Swiss on the way in and the reverse on the way back. Mady and Claude took me to Vallorbe several times. Vallorbe was the nearest town in Switzerland.

On one occasion Claude took Bordet and me to Les Verrières, the nearest border village. I don't think we had our passports with us. So Claude drove up to the French border post and parked his car there. We then decided to go for a walk in the forest. We set off uphill along the border and walked for about a kilometre through the forest. We then came to a clearing and continued to walk, in the snow, in the same direction. After a short while, we came across a man dressed like Robin Hood. The conversation was very good-natured, but the man explained to us that we were now in Switzerland and that he was a Swiss border-guard. Nevertheless, we were allowed to continue and went for a drink in a bar. We were also allowed to return to France without charge.

One Saturday evening early on in my stay a group of us went to Neuchatel for a *fondue*. *La fondue* is a typical Swiss dish. It is a mixture of Gruyère cheese and white wine, heated in a pot. Each participant has a fork and cubes of bread. The bread is dipped into the melted cheese and consumed along with suitable quantities of white wine. (In Switzerland, the standard measure for wine is the decilitre.)

I ate *fondues* on several occasions. The first couple of times I liked it, but after that it made me sick and I went off it. We quite often went out on Saturday evenings for a *gueuleton* or nosh-up. We usually went to a cheap restaurant and washed the food down with copious amounts of wine. As I have never liked being sick, I developed a knack of stopping drinking, just before I was going to feel ill. One evening in February, we went to a good restaurant, where I had my first taste of frogs' legs – very tasty, but not much of them! But the white Muscadet wine which went with them was delicious.

I joined a wrestling club with Robardet and someone else, but didn't enjoy it very much. It amused the man in charge, though: he was able to hold international wrestling contests.

Personal hygiene was a problem, though at 21 I was not over-concerned. The only way of having a bath or shower was by going to the public baths. They were situated in an old building just across the river at the bottom of the hill from where I lived. So, some Saturday afternoons (not many!) I took my towel and wash things and paid for a session in a bath cubicle.

I bought a transistor radio, which I kept in my room. I listened to *France Inter* and *Radio Suisse Romande*. Sacha Distel and *Les Compagnons de la Chanson* were very popular at that time. In spite of all the excitement I often got bored at the weekends.

During my time at Pontarlier I was supposed to do some reading in preparation for my final year at university. Before I left Manchester, I had had to choose a special subject for study in depth. Then, before the end of the Final year I would have to prepare a thesis of between 12000 and 15000 words. The subject I had chosen was "The Contemporary French novel". The authors to be studied were Camus, Malraux, Saint-Exupéry and Sartre. In my wisdom (or lack of it) I took the novels by Sartre with me to France. These included the first two volumes of *Les Chemins de la Liberté*, entitled *L'Age de Raison* and *le Sursis*. These are two of the most boring books I have ever read. Consequently it took me all year to read them and I read little else.

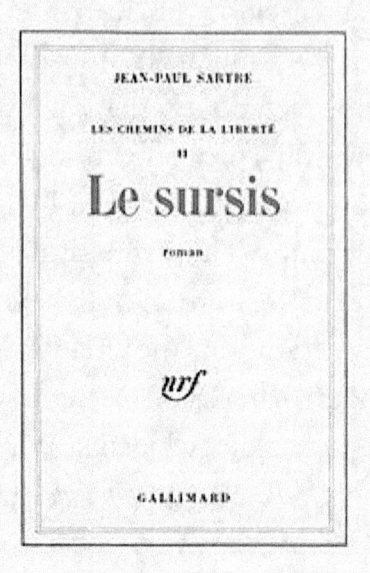

The following year, I expressed my criticism of *Le Sursis* to Graham Daniels, who was the tutor for the special subject. I said that for me a first requirement of a novel was that it should be comprehensible. In *Le Sursis* Sartre took a slice of time – the eight days before the signing of the Munich Agreement in 1938 – and explored the reactions of numerous characters to the possibility of war. He jumped without warning or preamble from one group to another, which made it very difficult, at least for me, to follow what was going on. Furthermore, as had been the case in *L'Age de Raison*, I found most of the characters unattractive. Graham Daniels replied with a knowing smile that *Le Sursis*, by looking at time vertically instead of horizontally, was considered to be an innovative novel.

Antibes

The CCCS invited me to go to Antibes for a fortnight at Easter 1961. This I was very pleased to accept. The *colonie* itself was not particularly memorable. We walked down to the *Port de la Salis* and on one occasion, we walked round the ramparts into the old town.

I went on two memorable excursions, probably on the same day. In the morning, we went to St Paul de Vence, a *village perché*, which had been converted, even then, into an up-market artists' paradise. On a fine day, which this was, it is as near to Paradise as most of us will ever get! Later, the coach took us along the *Moyenne Corniche* between Nice and Monaco. This is a road several hundred metres above sea-level with a sheer drop down to the Mediterranean below. It is a wonderful sight, but not quite so enjoyable if one is the driver, which I have been on several occasions since! We also went to Eze and saw the exotic cactus plants there.

St Paul de Vence

Eze

I then went on my own by coach to San Remo in Italy. Although I had tried to teach myself Italian, this was the only chance I had to go to Italy before I was nearly 40. It is more exotic than France. I particularly liked the flower-lined promenade there.

Back to Pontarlier

As I have mentioned earlier, the war in Algeria was at its height throughout this period. I went by coach to Besançon one Thursday in April to see Charles Baudard. In late afternoon, he insisted on accompanying me back to the coach station. This was partly because he wanted to see what was happening in one of the anti-Government demonstrations that were taking place all over France that day, including Besançon. We went to a café by the *Pont Battant*. A big and noisy demonstration was taking place in the square outside the café. The CRS riot police occupied the bridge, so that it was completely blocked. Anyone who stepped off the pavement was hit on the head by a truncheon. Frightening! I managed to get to the coach station unscathed, but one of the young *pions* was not so fortunate (or careful) and ended up in hospital. This was the day that I discovered that French policemen were not at all like English bobbies!

On 21st April 1961, a number of French generals revolted and took control of Algeria. It was feared that they would seek to invade mainland France. De Gaulle once again took to the airwaves in full military uniform and made an impassioned plea to the French population, which ended *Françaises, Français ! Aidez-moi !* He also declared a state of emergency, giving himself supreme power until 30th September. Meanwhile in Pontarlier, there was concern that the invasion might land at the airstrip on the outskirts of the town. A group of vigilantes, led by Monsieur Blondeau, spent one or two nights at the airstrip, keeping watch in case the invaders landed there. They didn't! Blondeau was a big, bearded man, who was a teacher at our school. He was a member of the French Communist Party and a deputy mayor of Pontarlier.

Not many of my colleagues at the school were particularly politically minded, but those that were, were of a left-wing persuasion. A new political party, the *Parti Socialiste Unifié*, was formed, led by Pierre Mendès-France. Gaudet was a member and I found his ideas quite attractive. Marcel Queney was also a socialist, but he remained faithful to the traditional socialist party led by Guy Mollet.

One weekend Marcel and a couple of other teachers took a group of senior pupils to Montana in Switzerland. They invited me to go with them. We stayed in a good hotel, but, as it was low season, it was reasonably priced. Montana is a fashionable resort – several steps up-market from Pontarlier. On the Saturday evening, I went out with the pupils. Marcel said on the Sunday morning that he was pleased I had done so, because I had been able to keep an eye on them. I am not sure that the compliment was accurate, but no harm was done. A famous British author was staying in the same hotel with a lady friend. I think her name was Nancy Sears, but I am not sure.

There are many public holidays in France in May. The dates of most French holidays are fixed, so, if it falls on a Tuesday, Wednesday or Thursday, people often make the bridge to the nearest weekend.

One weekend I decided to take my bike as far as I could westwards and then get the train back. Accordingly I rode to Autun. I am sorry to say that I don't remember anything more about that journey. That was to be the last bike ride of any significance in this story.

A few weeks later, I was much more ambitious. I decided to hitch-hike as far as I could in a south-westerly direction. I had no destination in mind and certainly not the one I ended up in. My lifts took me across the Saône to Paray-le-Monial, which I recollect as being in a mining area, but I can find no evidence to support that. The next day I went to Vichy. During the war Vichy had been the capital of the French State, but by this time it had reverted to being a quiet, but opulent, spa town. I saw a snake on the bridge there, but it slithered away harmlessly.

I got a lift to the outskirts of Clermont-Ferrand. From there, I got a lift with a taciturn lorry-driver, who was going to Alès, nearly 300 kilometres away. He asked me to give him directions. I had my map. I could see that about 40 km south of Clermont, the road forked and we needed to take the left fork. Unfortunately, when we got there, I missed it and we took the road to Montpellier instead. It was some time before we realised that I had made a mistake. The lorry driver was not amused, but there was no way he could turn his big lorry round on those narrow windy roads. The first opportunity to get back on a main road to Alès was at Mende, nearly 150 kilometres from Clermont. So we went about 50 kilometres out of our way.

It was one of the most beautiful journeys I ever went on. It would have been late spring. The sun was shining. The earth was dry. There were hardly any trees, just scrub-like bushes. Very little human habitation, just miles and miles of open mountainous countryside. Eventually, we went through the towns of Mende and Florac. I remember thinking that this would be the most beautiful place to spend one's life and that I would go back there. I hardly ever did! I think I realised even then, that there wouldn't be much for me actually to do there.

Eventually we arrived at Alès in late afternoon, some 500 kilometres from Pontarlier by a direct route. Alès is not the ideal holiday destination. But it was warm and sunny and it was the south of France: the nearest well-known towns are Avignon and

Nimes. And it did have a citadel built by Vauban! I spent most of the next day sitting in the sun reading a book.

The following day I started my journey back to Pontarlier. I got a lift to St. Etienne. This took me on another scenic journey through the Cévennes. In particular I went near to the Puy de Dôme, a spectacular extinguished volcano.

Le Puy de Dôme

I was bowled over by St Etienne. If I went back there now, I suspect I would find it to be a rather uninteresting industrial town. On that day it encapsulated many of my experiences to date. As I was driven into the city, it was nearly dark. The journey through the dreary suburbs reminded me of a similar journey I had made into Nottingham. The hills around the city reminded me of Besançon. The smell of coffee, when I walked outside the hotel the following morning reminded me of Paris. … And then there was the sunshine and warmth of southern France. I wrote a poem while I was there. Fortunately I can only remember the first line, because the rest doesn't sound very promising:

Saint-Etienne : Ville de mes rêves !

The next day, I travelled back to Pontarlier. I had arranged to meet Mady and Claude on that Thursday evening, so I had a tight timetable. All went well in the morning, but I got stuck in the afternoon at Lons le Saulnier. I went along to the station, but there were no convenient trains. So, I went back on to the road and thumbed more frantically than usual. It worked!

Towards the end of my stay in Pontarlier, a new *pion* came to the school. His name was Jean-Claude Boutonnet. He was calmer and more mature than most of the other *pions*. I got on very well with him. He also came from Besançon and had a widowed mother. He didn't stay at Pontarlier very long. When he left he said that he was going to study to become a civil servant.

In 1976 – fifteen years later – I was privileged to go on a course at the *Ecole Nationale d'Administration (ENA)* in Paris.

This was the institution where all the top civil servants and most government ministers go to complete their education. One day I asked if Jean-Claude had been there. He hadn't, but the person I asked had a government directory. Jean-Claude was a senior official in the French senate. He later became Director of Finance, one of the most senior non-elected officials in that organisation. I got in touch with him and so a beautiful friendship was resumed. He had a house in Palaiseau on the outskirts of Paris. We have visited him – and his wife, Odette, and their three children on several occasions. They also invited our elder son, Peter, to go on holiday with them to their holiday home in the Alps, which he did on two occasions. When Jean-Claude became Director, they were given an official apartment in Rue Bonaparte, just round the corner from the *Palais Luxembourg*, where he worked.

He has showed us round the *Palais Luxembourg* on a number of occasions. It is one of the most beautiful buildings I have ever visited and I would not hesitate to visit again, if I were given the opportunity. On the last occasion – I would have been about 69 at the time – he took us to the restaurant which the senators use. He could not have done that if the Senate had been sitting, but they weren't. There was an old man sitting in the corner – considerably older than I thought I was! Jean-Claude introduced me to him, as a retired civil servant at the Senate. It turned out that this "old man" had been one of my pupils at Pontarlier.

Jean-Claude in a Senate meeting room 2009

On that occasion Odette told me about Jean-Claude's early life. I had known that he had gone to the *lycée* at Besançon and that one of his friends there had been Jean-Pierre Chevènement who had gone on to be a senior minister in successive Socialist governments. But I was shocked to learn that Jean-Claude's father had been in the French Resistance and had been executed towards the end of the war.

Belley

My contract at Pontarlier expired at the end of June 1961. I bought a new suitcase, in which I put all my most important belongings. I packed everything else in my trunk and despatched it by rail, along with my bike, back to my home in Wymeswold.

I arranged with the CCCS to work as a *moniteur* in their *colonie de vacances* at Belley, which was in the *Ain* department, about half-way between Lyon and Geneva. Geologically it was in the south of the Jura range.

I set out by train from Pontarlier and arrived at Lyon Perrache station in the early afternoon. It was the first time I had been to Lyon and it was very hot. (It was always hot when I went to Lyon!) I had to walk across the centre of Lyon to get a coach to Belley. There were not many other people on the coach, but it was still very hot. Eventually I arrived and made the way to the *colonie*, which was in the *lycée de Belley*; from the front this was very similar to the *lycée de Pontarlier*!

There was nothing very special about Belley, but this was the *colonie*, which I enjoyed the most. That was, in no small part due to the Director, Paulette Cuny, and her husband, Robert, who was the *économe* in charge of the administration. They had two boys; Christian was about 10 years old, Pierre was five or six.

Once more I arrived a few days before the children, which gave me an opportunity to learn my way about, beforehand. I also made a conscious effort to be more assertive, as no-one I would meet there knew anything about me. I remember going with Robert to a local farm on a hill-top just outside Belley. The farmer made a very pleasant rosé wine. Robert bought some for the staff to drink. He complained later that, because it was good, we were drinking too much of it and threatened to buy *gros rouge* instead, if we didn't reduce our consumption. I don't know whether we did or not, but, fortunately, the threat was never carried out.

We had a good team of *moniteurs*. The chaps were housed in small dormitories across a courtyard from the main building.

Near the *Col des Aravis, July 1961*
Back row: Yvette, Paulette, ?, ?, me, Louisette, 2 kitchen staff; !?
Front row: Robert, Pierre, ?, Christian, Monique, Jacky

We worked and played well together and I think Paulette and Robert were pleased with us. I was quite fond of Monique, an auburn-haired *Bretonne* from Quimperlé. I pursued her mercilessly throughout the month (and very briefly a year later!) We got on well together and spent at least one day off together. The only tangible reward for my endeavours was one brief kiss. She said later that she regretted it, because it only encouraged me to be more persistent!

I also remember Louisette very well. She was the *infirmière*.

She was a big fair-haired girl, with a strong personality, but whom we teased a lot. She and I had the reputation for being the strictest members of staff.

Once again, I had younger boys, including Pierre Cuny, Paulette's younger son. The boys were fairly well-behaved, though many of them came from poor Parisian families.

There wasn't a lot to do in Belley. It was then a town with some 6000 inhabitants. Its main claim to fame was as the birthplace of Jean Anthelme Brillat-Savarin (1755 to 1826). He was a lawyer and politician, who gained fame as an epicure and writer on gastronomy. He was an early advocate of a low-carbohydrate diet. This was, however, of little interest to me or my children. There was a "stadium" in the town, which we went to once or twice. All I remember about that is that it was a long walk to get there and very hot when we did get there. Nevertheless for the most part, we occupied the children with games and songs in and around the school.

One of the routines in all the *colonies* was the siesta in the early afternoon. This is a challenging time for the *moniteurs* as one has to try to get twenty or thirty boys to lie down and keep quiet, when they would prefer to be running around making a noise. Nevertheless, at Belley at least, I was quite good at it. I thought about that experience over 40 years later, when I had great difficulty getting one or two granddaughters to calm down and go to sleep!

We did go on some good excursions from Belley. In particular we went to one or more of the beautiful Savoy lakes and recalled Lamartine's poem, which was set in the *Lac du Bourget*.

Le Lac

Ainsi toujours poussés vers de nouveaux rivages,
Dans la nuit éternelle emportés sans retour,
Ne pourrons-nous jamais sur l'océan des âges
Jeter l'ancre un seul jour?

O lac! l'année à peine a fini sa carrière,
Et près des flots chéris qu'elle devait revoir
Regarde! Je viens seul m'asseoir sur cette pierre
Où tu la vis s'asseoir!

Tu mugissais ainsi sous ces roches profondes;
Ainsi tu te brisais sur leurs flancs déchirés:
Ainsi le vent jetait l'écume de tes ondes
Sur ses pieds adorés.

Un soir, t'en souvient-il ? nous voguions en silence;
On n'entendait au loin, sur l'onde et sous les cieux,
Que le bruit des rameurs qui frappaient en cadence
Tes flots harmonieux.

Tout à coup des accents inconnus à la terre
Du rivage charmé frappèrent les échos;
Le flot fut attentif, et la voix qui m'est chère
Laissa tomber ces mots:

"O temps, suspends ton vol! et vous, heures propices,
Suspendez votre cours!
Laissez-nous savourer les rapides délices
Des plus beaux de nos jours!

"Assez de malheureux ici-bas vous implorent:
Coulez, coulez pour eux;
Prenez avec leurs jours les soins qui les dévorent;
Oubliez les heureux.

"Mais je demande en vain quelques moments encore,
Le temps m'échappe et fuit;
Je dis à cette nuit: "Sois plus lente"; et l'aurore
Va dissiper la nuit.

"Aimons donc, aimons donc! de l'heure fugitive,
Hâtons-nous, jouissons!
L'homme n'a point de port, le temps n'a point de rive;
Il coule, et nous passons!"

Temps jaloux, se peut-il que ces moments d'ivresse,
Où l'amour à longs flots nous verse le bonheur,
S'envolent loin de nous de la même vitesse
Que les jours de malheur?

Hé quoi! N'en pourrons-nous fixer au moins la trace?
Quoi! Passés pour jamais? Quoi! Tout entiers perdus?
Ce temps qui les donna, ce temps qui les efface,
Ne nous les rendra plus?

Éternité, néant, passé, sombres abîmes,
Que faites-vous des jours que vous engloutissez?
Parlez: nous rendrez-vous ces extases sublimes
Que vous nous ravissez?

O lac! Rochers muets! Grottes! Forêt obscure!
Vous que le temps épargne ou qu'il peut rajeunir,
Gardez de cette nuit, gardez, belle nature,
Au moins le souvenir!

Qu'il soit dans ton repos, qu'il soit dans tes orages,
Beau lac, et dans l'aspect de tes riants coteaux,
Et dans ces noirs sapins, et dans ces rocs sauvages
Qui pendent sur tes eaux!

I Went There on my Bike

Qu'il soit dans le zéphyr qui frémit et qui passe,
Dans les bruits de tes bords par tes bords répétés,
Dans l'astre au front d'argent qui blanchit ta surface
De ses molles clartés!

Que le vent qui gémit, le roseau qui soupire,
Que les parfums légers de ton air embaumé,
Que tout ce qu'on entend, l'on voit ou l'on respire,
Tout dise: "Ils ont aimé!"

Le Lac du Bourget

We also went to the Alps, in particular to the *Col des Aravis*, an impressive mountain pass at an altitude of almost 1500 metres.

Le Col des Aravis

On one of my days off, I went with Monique to *La Mer de Glace*, an impressive, though disappointingly dirty, glacier reached from Chamonix.

Chamonix

Plouha

At the end of my stay at Belley, I packed my suitcase and went by coach, along with some other *moniteurs* and most of the children to Ambérieu. There we got a train to Paris. The plan was to spend the night in Paris and then I would travel the next day to Plouha in northern Britanny, where I had arranged to work in another CCCS *colonie* for the month of August.

It was a long train journey to Paris and it was late evening, when we arrived at the *Gare de Lyon*. I was quite tired. From there I got on the coach, which took me, along with a coach-load of other young adults to the well-appointed hostel accommodation, where I was due to spend the night. I sat near the back and, I thought, I put my suit-case on the back seat of the coach. When we arrived at our destination, a young man, accompanied by a young woman, picked up the suit-case, got off the coach and started carrying it towards the accommodation. I followed him and, after a few yards, I thanked him and said I could carry my own suitcase. He replied that it was not my suitcase, but his. I went back to where the coach had dropped us, but it had already left. I instigated enquiries through CCCS, but I never saw my suit-case again.

You may recall that, when I left Pontarlier, I put all the most important things in the suit-case and sent the rest of my things back to Wymeswold in my trunk. The trunk arrived safely, but not the suit-case. Apart from clothes, the case contained all my university notes (which I would need for the Final Examinations) and the pen which my parents had bought me for my 21st birthday. I was very upset.

Soon after I arrived at Plouha, I went to the local market and bought a minimum of clothes, including a grey pullover, which I kept for many years.

The *colonie* at Plouha was situated about a kilometre from the coast and a few kilometres west of the town of St. Brieuc, which was where my friend, Jean, from Biarritz came from. We went there on a number of occasions.

The atmosphere at the *colonie* was very different to that at Belley. Everyone called the Director, *Tonton Louis*. He was a big man, with a big personality. Whereas Belley had been quiet and orderly, Plouha was noisy and somewhat chaotic. So, we had a lively time. There were two English *monitrices* there. They were the first English people I had spoken to for eleven months.

There was a pleasant walk along country paths to the beach. We also went on two or three excursions, including past the pink rocks of Perros Guirec and the island of Bréhat. The trip to the latter was one of the best days of my life. It is a small island, with, then at least, no cars. We walked around the island in peace on a beautiful August day. That was the day, when I realised that I liked islands. Subsequently I have spent many of my most enjoyable days on islands: the Scilly Islands, where we went for our honeymoon and three times since, Sark, Inhaca and the *Iles des Lérins*, in particular.

Perros-Guirec

Bréhat

Manchester 3

After an uninterrupted absence of eleven months, I returned to England at the end of August 1961. Before I left Plouha, I received a letter from my father to say that I needed to go to the customs at Newhaven to import my bike. Accordingly, I travelled back home via Dieppe and Newhaven. On arrival at Newhaven, I was able to go along to the Customs House, complete the formalities and still catch my train to Victoria. My bike then went on its way to Loughborough Midland station.

When I arrived home in Wymeswold, my mother said they wanted to buy me a "proper" 21st birthday present. I decided I would like a transistor radio, the one I had in Pontarlier having been lost in my suit-case in Paris. At that time, we expected to pay about £14 for a radio, equivalent to a good weekly wage for a highly skilled worker. Accordingly we got on the bus to Nottingham. We went into a shop in the Old Market Square. There was a sale in the shop and they had a mahogany radiogram on offer for £21. This was a "piece of furniture" and, from my mother's point of view, a much better present than a mere transistor radio. So she bought it and it was delivered to Wymeswold.

I was not very knowledgeable about music, but I decided that I ought to buy some records to play on the radiogram. Accordingly I bought 45rpm records by Acker Bilk and Chris Barber. Fairly soon thereafter, I acquired LPs by Beethoven and Tchaikovsky. A little later – I don't remember how – I acquired EPs by Gilbert Bécaud, Yves Montand and Georges Brassens. I later acquired some records by Edith Piaf and the Shadows, but that was about all I had for many years.

During the month of September, Margaret Lifetree came to see me. She was staying with her parents in West Bridgford,

Nottingham. She had been on the same course as me at Manchester for the first two years, but had returned in October 1960 to complete her degree. She had then decided to apply to work as an *assistante* in France. She had been allocated to … the *lycée de Pontarlier*! I gave her all the information I could, but I couldn't help thinking that the *pions* at Pontarlier would tease her unmercifully.

The radiogram was transported to Manchester (along with my bike). Bryn James had got his degree – a B.A. Honours Degree (2.i) in French Studies. He had enrolled in the Education Department for a one-year course to obtain a post-graduate Teaching Diploma. We decided to get a flat together. He found one at 14 Swinbourne Grove, Withington. The flat was on the top floor of a Victorian house. We had two reasonable-sized rooms: a living room with a kitchen area behind a curtain and a bedroom with two single beds. [I have just looked up the address on the internet and a modern care home has been built on the site.]

The flat was well situated. Withington was a pleasant suburb and there were a number of buses that went along Wilmslow Road straight to the University. Bryn and I continued to get on well together. We each put an equal amount of money in a kitty and bought food and other essentials from the kitty. I don't remember us ever having a serious row about anything.

My private life took a turn for the better. I went back to the Saturday evening dances in the Students' Union, which still followed the same format as three years earlier. The boys wore suits and ties. The girls wore pretty dresses. One of these girls was called Margaret Coleman. She was a pretty Irish girl, with dark hair and blue eyes. She came from Lisburn in Northern Ireland, but, at that time her father was stationed at Wymondham in

Norfolk. She was a year older than me and was studying for her final year in Chemistry. We met at one of the dances in October 1961.

I was terrified at that time of being sued for "breach of contract". I made it clear, right from the start that I did not want a permanent relationship. I was, nevertheless, invited round to her digs in the evenings in Levenshulme, where we indulged in heavy petting, along with two or three other couples under the benign surveillance of the youngish landlady. This was the early sixties, however, and there was never any question of "going further".

We spent most Saturday evenings and Sundays together, but hardly ever met in between. The relationship lasted until we both left Manchester in June 1962. I arranged to go to Wymondham to meet her parents just after Christmas. I was a little uneasy about this, but, conveniently, I caught a bad cold and decided I wasn't fit to travel. Modern technology had reached both our parents' houses, so I was able to telephone her. She was not best pleased. Her displeasure was compounded by the fact that Danièle Borgazzi, who was studying in England at the time, came to stay with us for a few days in Wymeswold. Even if I had wanted to, Danièle was not the sort to permit any "shilly-shallying", but Margaret remained unconvinced by that argument.

Bryn also kept me on the straight and narrow. He had a long-term relationship with his girl-friend from his home in Sheffield, Christine, which he maintained was chaste. He also made it clear that he would not approve of any inappropriate behaviour in our flat. By this time, Christine was at Teachers' Training College at Warrington. The four of us went out for walks in the Derbyshire Dales on a few occasions.

Most of the people that had been on the same course as me in the first two years at Manchester had completed their course, though many of them, like Bryn, had stayed on to do a Teaching Diploma. But I made new friends and life carried on as before.

I did not return to the Manchester Football Association as a referee. I did, however, referee a couple of matches "for" the French Society. I was still very young looking. On one occasion I got on a bus at Withington togged up in my football gear and the bus conductor charged me half fare (i.e. under fourteen). I was 22 at the time. A similar thing happened to me two or three years later. Jennifer, my fiancée at the time, and I walked from Wymeswold to Hoton two miles away. We stopped for a drink at the Packe Arms. That, incidentally, had been the pub where I had had my first half pint of mild beer – it cost me 7 pence halfpenny – when I was seventeen years old. When I went with Jennifer the landlord asked us whether we were old enough: I was nearly 25, Jennifer was 20!

Having just completed his final year successfully, Bryn was in a strong position to lecture me on what I needed to do in order to get a good degree. And he did! He also lent me his university notes, because I had lost mine in my suit-case. They were better than mine! Following his advice, I resolved to work for nine hours a day, Monday to Friday: three hours in the morning, three in the afternoon, and three in the evening. I carried out this programme religiously throughout the University year.

In the day-time, I did my private study in the Arts Library, usually in the stacks. As I said earlier, these looked out on to poor back-to-back houses in the Hulme district of Manchester. It was strange to go back after eighteen months to see the same poor dog barking in the back "garden" of one of the houses.

The Library was closed in the evening. I went instead to the Students' Union, which had a quiet room on the top floor; this was open until 10 o'clock. There were two related problems with it: it was very warm; and I had a tendency to fall asleep.

This had already become a problem in France, beginning in Besançon, but exacerbated in Pontarlier. Whenever I went to the cinema there, I almost invariably went to sleep. From time to time Marcel Queney and others organised evening lectures in the school, all of which I went to. Most of them were very interesting. One was on Teilhard de Chardin, which I found particularly interesting. But it didn't stop me going to sleep! In Pontarlier, this had been a minor embarrassment, but in Manchester, it presented a serious threat to the achievement of my work programme. At first I tried to fight against it, but after a time I decided that it was better to allow myself to fall asleep for twenty minutes or so and then carry on refreshed.

I decided that I needed to re-read all the books on the literature courses at least once, which I think I did, though I can't imagine that I re-opened *Le Sursis*. Consequently, whereas it had taken me eighteen months to read two books, I was now reading some of the shorter books, like *La Porte Etroite* by Gide, in two days.

Towards the end of 1961, I was persuaded to subscribe to a special volume of *Studies in French Literature* which was presented to Professor P Mansell Jones. The cost was 42 shillings – a not insignificant sum in those days. It contained 27 essays, including one by my tutor, Graham Daniels, entitled 'The sense of the past in the novels of Malraux'.[2] The volume has my name in it, along with other subscribers.[3]

---

[2] Other contributors from Manchester were: L.J. Austin, Anne Churchman, Gilbert Gadoffre, Jean Gaudon, F.W. Saunders, F.E. Sutcliffe and Eugène Vinaver.

[3] These include the following members of staff not mentioned above: Fanni Bogdanow, W Mansfield Cooper (Vice-Chancellor), GE Gwynne, N Hampson, Elspeth Kennedy and Frederick Whitehead; and the following student contemporaries: Howard Abbott, Michael Buckby, Jeffrey Coulthard and GR Murray – quite a select band, really! (I was at Loughborough Grammar School with Graham Murray; Mike Buckby and Jeff Coulthard were at Besançon with me.)

The Final examination had a number of elements, each of which had one three-hour written examination at the end, and each with equal marks. We also had to write a thesis on our special subject. Finally there was an oral examination, which was only used in borderline situations. There was only a very limited choice of broad options. The only subject that I had chosen not to take at the beginning of the second year had been Morphology and Phonology. The subjects I did take were French History (taken at the end of the second year) Syntax and Semantics (based on lectures at the beginning of the first or second year, translation to and from French and English, a dissertation, Old French, Poetry, Drama and Novels and the special subject.

For the dissertation examination, we studied three authors: Montaigne, Descartes and Pascal. Professor Sutcliffe, a forbidding Yorkshireman, lectured us each week in preparation for this. He rattled out his lectures at a fast dictation speed. All we could do was to sit there and write down as much as we could. I had the advantage that I also had Bryn's notes to fall back on, if I couldn't understand my own.

The set book for Old French was *La Chanson de Roland*, the story of Charlemagne's foray into Spain to fight against the infidel Moors. As mentioned earlier, in the first two years we had learned the basics of mediaeval French grammar and read *La Chastelaine de Vergi*, which was written in the thirteenth century in a purer form of French. *La Chanson de Roland* was written two centuries earlier and was therefore more difficult to understand – but we managed!

We also had lectures on François Villon, Rabelais, and the *Pléiade* poets, though I don't now remember where they fitted in. I liked all of these, in particular Villon, a fourteenth century reprobate, who recounted his misdeeds in long poems. One of his most famous lines is: *Où sont les neiges d'antan?* 'Where are the snows of yester-year?'

Dr Elspeth Kennedy was the lecturer on Rabelais. She was a middle-aged woman with protruding teeth. She was an unlikely-looking person for the purveyance of more earthy stories. The main thing I can remember about her lectures is the way she pronounced the 'R' in Rabelais. She tried to reproduce the guttural French 'r', but sounded as though she was trying to cough up some nasty substance from her bronchial tubes. Nevertheless the stories of Gargantua and Pantagruel appealed to my juvenile sense of humour. He was given the name Gargantua, because his father, Grandgousier, looked at him after he had been born out of his mother, Gargamelle's, ear, saw that he was big and exclaimed to her: *Que grand tu as!* His father's name, like his mother's, is fairly easy to interpret. I particularly liked Rabelais' explanation of the origin of the word 'Beauce', which is a productive agricultural area in the centre of France. Gargantua was riding through the area on his horse, when he exclaimed: *Est beau ce !*

For all three literature courses, the prospectus read the same each year: *There are no set books, but the following are recommended.* There followed a long list of authors. A fairly cursory inspection of previous examination papers revealed that there were usually one or two questions on each of the authors listed. In order to make the most efficient use of time, I decided to concentrate on three authors in each category, with a fourth in reserve in case I couldn't answer the question on one of my chosen authors.

For Drama I chose Corneille, Racine, Beaumarchais and Marivaux. Under the distant guidance of Professor Vinaver, I became quite an expert on Racine.

As I was a slow reader and my special subject included many long novels, length was my main criterion for the choice of texts to study. So I chose the shortest ones I could find: *La Princesse de Clèves* (Madame de La Fayette), *Adolphe* (Benjamin Constant, *René* by Chateaubriand and *L'Immoraliste* and *La Porte Etroite* by André Gide. Much to my surprise, I really liked *La Princesse de Clèves*, which was a 17th century novel with many of the classical attributes of Racine's plays. I also liked Gide very much.

I chose the poems of Ronsard, Baudelaire and Mallarmé with Leconte de Lisle as my fourth option. I particularly liked Ronsard's poetry. The choice of Mallarmé was a bold one. His poetry is *very* difficult to understand. So I decided that I either had to put a lot of work into studying him or leave him alone. I decided to put the work in. Having said that, I don't think I ever had an original thought on his work, but I learned pretty thoroughly what other people had written about it. The recommended poems were all reproduced in *Modern French Verse: An Anthology*.[4]

> FRENCH CLASSICS
> General Editor: EUGÈNE VINAVER
>
> ## MODERN FRENCH VERSE
>
> AN ANTHOLOGY
>
> with an Introduction
>
> *by*
>
> P. MANSELL JONES
>
> MANCHESTER UNIVERSITY PRESS

The Mallarmé poems were:

Apparition

Brise Marine

Toast Funèbre

O si chère de loin et proche et blanche

Victorieusement fui le suicide beau

Le vierge, le vivace et le bel aujourd'hui

Le Tombeau d'Edgar Poe

Toute l'âme résumée.

---

[4] *Modern French Verse: An Anthology* with an introduction by P.Mansell Jones, a retired professor at Manchester University, general editor: Eugène Vinaver, published by Manchester University Press, 1954, price 7s/6d. The poets included were: Gérard de Nerval, Charles Baudelaire, Stéphane Mallarmé, Paul Verlaine, Tristan Corbière, Arthur Rimbaud, Emile Verhaeren, Jean Moréas, Jules Laforgue, Charles van Lerberghe, Maurice Maeterlinck, Henri de Régnier, Francis Vielé-Griffin, Francis Jammes, Paul Claudel, Paul Valéry and Guillaume Apollinaire.

I found detailed critiques of all the poems in that selection, save one. An inspection of previous examination papers revealed that each year there was a question requiring an *explication de texte* of one poem in the selection. A more detailed inspection revealed that over the previous seven years there had been a question on each of the poems in the selection for which I had found a critique. I forecast correctly that the eighth poem would come up in 1962. I also knew that, if it did, I wouldn't be able to answer the question, because I had not been able to find a critique of it. Nevertheless, I told myself that it would be in my interest, if the other question on Mallarmé in the final examination was difficult, because I thought I would be better prepared than most. It so happened that the poetry examination was the very last examination I sat. There was only one day when I had two three-hour examinations on the same day, but that was it! When I saw the question, my heart sank: it was *too* difficult. Nevertheless, I managed to write something. I can still remember that warm June afternoon, singing silently to myself: *I'm tired and I want to go to bed!*

Thanks to Mallarmé, by the end of the year, everything had come together in my head. I formed a clear idea of what constituted true literature and what was mere writing. There existed a Platonic Ideal. The closer writers and other artists could get to that ideal, the more they produced true art. Ronsard, Racine, Baudelaire, Mallarmé, T.S. Eliot, D.H. Lawrence among others were able to do that; C.P. Snow, who was a literary *bête noire* at the time, definitely did not.

The *pièce de résistance* of this final year was the thesis. This had to be between 12,000 and 15,000 words long and had to be typed. After some hesitation I plumped for Saint-Exupéry.

I then knew what I wanted to write about, but struggled to find the right title. Eventually I settled for *Saint-Exupéry and the Meaning of Human Existence*. I am still quite proud of the way I organised my writing. This being long before the days of word-processors, I decided to write one or two paragraphs on one sheet of paper. This meant that I could move the paragraphs around, if I wanted to. It also meant that, if I wanted to change something, I had only half a page or so to rewrite, rather than "messing up" a number of pages. Jennifer has retyped the thesis and I have reproduced it as an annex to this document.

When it came to sitting the Final examinations I was well prepared and fairly relaxed. The first examination was on *Syntax and Semantics*. The examination took place on a fine late spring day. It was held in the Whitworth Art Gallery, just along the road from the Arts Building. I remember writing what I thought were amusing examples to illustrate the difference between connotations and denotations.

All that was to change the following day. Our itinerary took us that afternoon to a new Science or Mathematics building on the opposite side of Oxford Road. It was a hot day and the room we were in was on a high floor and had a lot of windows. We were there for three hours to write a dissertation in French. We were well drilled in the rules for writing a dissertation, which were much more constraining than those for an English essay. And we had all carefully studied our notes from Professor Sutcliffe's lectures. An inspection of previous years' papers revealed that there had always been two questions on Descartes, two on Pascal and one on Montaigne. As with most other subjects I concentrated on one of the three: Pascal's *Pensées*. The examination papers were distributed. As far as I can remember there was only one question relating to Pascal. We were mostly working-class lads and lasses from the Midlands and North of England. The question (in French) was something about the beauty of the thought. What on earth was that all about? I was usually good at written examinations. But then, for the first and only time in my life, I just panicked and froze (I don't remember in which order). For a full half hour I just sat there and wrote nothing. I looked round and saw that most of my colleagues were in the same boat. I then sat down and wrote something and handed it in at the end of the three hours. I seem to remember that at least one of my fellow students gave up the contest long before that.

That was, of course, a wake-up call. I realised that from then on I was playing catch-up and that I couldn't afford any more slip-ups. I don't remember anything about the remaining examinations until the last one, which I have already described.

The results of the examinations were put up on a notice board some days later. Throughout the final year at least, and possibly longer, I had realised that I was working hard to get an Upper Second Bachelor of Arts Honours Degree in French Studies (Second Class Division One or "two-one" in the vernacular). My analysis was as follows. People who were really clever and worked got Firsts: there were three or four of them out of 70; we knew who they were and I was not one of them. The really clever people who didn't work generally got two-twos. The vast majority of ordinary mortals got a two-one if they worked and a two-two or very occasionally a Third Class Degree if they didn't. (I think there was only one in my year.) There were two further categories: an Ordinary Degree and failure. I think there was one Ordinary Degree in my year and one failure in the year before – one of the chaps, who started at the same time as I did. These three are interesting case studies.

In the case of Barry who got a third, it was a bit of a shock and disappointment. He was a very sociable chap – I used to play table tennis with him. Like me, he had done a year in France, so he spoke good French. He was reasonably intelligent. He obviously didn't work too hard, but didn't give the impression of a layabout. I think, in the end, he probably didn't have the exam technique.

I don't think the same excuses could be made for Geoff. He was intelligent, but played harder than he worked. He was never short of female admirers. He had an easy manner and a good fluent turn of phrase. He had many more job offers than all the rest of us.

Dave was a disappointment. He was a big lad from the West Midlands with a matching personality. He came to Manchester in 1958 with a County Major Scholarship. From the start, he consumed large quantities of beer and other alcoholic beverages. He used to recite a ditty in a West Country accent:

I likes cider
Cider makes I fat
When I'm fat I'm happy
When I'm happy, I drinks more cider
I likes cider …

He went to one or two lectures in the first few weeks at University. After that, someone else signed in for Dave and he was never seen in lectures again. I was still in France when he completed his three-year stay in Manchester. I was told that the authorities pleaded with him to write "something" for his thesis, so that they could award a degree, but he declined to do so.

I don't know where the results of the Final examination were posted, but I remember the moment of ecstatic relief when I read that I had indeed got a two-one. I immediately hugged a female fellow student, who had also got a two-one. I told the vicar of Wymeswold sometime later that I had got a two-one. He said that was what he got too and added that the beauty of that is that you can always think that you might nearly have got a first. I dismissed that at the time, but on occasions since, I have thought well, maybe, I wasn't far off getting a first. This pipe dream is reinforced by a conversation I had some years later with my tutor, Graham Daniels. I went to enquire about doing an MA on my own. I asked Graham whether my degree was good enough. He replied that they would only refuse if my degree was borderline two-two, "which was certainly not the case with you". (For the record, I started the MA under the direction of Professor Gilbert Gadoffre, but didn't get very far.)

My parents came to Manchester for the degree award ceremony. They stayed with Uncle Will and Aunt Alice in Barlow Moor Road, Chorlton-cum-Hardy. We got a bus from there to All Saints' Square. On the way back, there was a queue for the bus and my father nearly got left behind. I think his only recollection of the day was of me shouting to the bus conductor: "Don't forget my Dad!"

THE VICTORIA
UNIVERSITY OF MANCHESTER

Degree of

Bachelor of Arts

It is hereby certified that

James William Mackley

satisfied the Examiners in the Final Examination for the above-
named Degree with Honours in the subject of *French Studies*
being placed in the *Second* Class, Division *I* and has been duly
admitted as a BACHELOR OF ARTS of this University.

Registrar.

Getting a job

Fairly early on in my final year, it occurred to me, and most of my friends, that at the end of the year we were going to have to go out in the big wide world and get a job. The idea of staying on for another year or two to get a Master's Degree did cross my mind, but only briefly at that point. For one thing, I did not think I was good enough – it never occurred to me to ask! More pertinently, having had a job in Pontarlier with a comfortable salary, I had had enough of the student existence. (Nevertheless a year later I would look back with envy on those golden years!)

The obvious option was to go into teaching. Accordingly, along with many of my colleagues, I applied to the Education Department to do a one-year Teaching Diploma. This was the same course as Bryn James was doing. I was accepted for interview. Most of my colleagues really wanted to do this course and were very nervous. I had more or less made up my mind that that was not what I wanted to do. Consequently I was not at all nervous and had one of the best interviews I ever had. I was offered a place, but declined it.

Having burnt that particular boat, I went along to the University Appointments Board and had an interview with the head man, Mr Holloway. (My memory tells me his name was Stanley, but I fear that my memory may be playing tricks on me!) Having asked me a few questions, his first suggestion was: *What about the Home Civil Service?* To which I replied: *No way!*

There were about seventy of us at Manchester University and similar numbers at dozens of universities round the country. Most of us wanted jobs "where we could use our languages".

Outside teaching, such jobs were few and far between. Whether or not I could use my languages, I wanted to be able to travel abroad. I bought a thick book entitled *Directory of Opportunities for Graduates*. This listed all the companies with graduate recruitment schemes. I applied to some of them.

I went for an interview at Coates at Glasgow. Before I went any further I was asked to do a colour-blindness test. As the firm dealt in cotton, it would have been pointless to carry on if I couldn't distinguish between the different colours. I passed the test, but wasn't offered a job.

I also went for an interview with Kalamazoo in Birmingham. I then went for an interview with BOAC (British Overseas Air Corporation) at Heathrow airport. My experience of airports at that time was limited to tiny aerodromes at Beauvais and Lympne in Kent. Even in 1962 Heathrow appeared huge to me – it even had its own telephone exchange with a dedicated prefix. It was a warm day. When I eventually reached the interview room, I was hot and sweaty. There were several people on the panel, most of whom had their backs to a window through which the sun was shining brightly. I was invited to sit facing the window. This was possibly designed to see how I reacted to pressure. Not very well, it seems. I was not surprised not to be offered a job.

My final interview in this context was with the Bata Shoe Company. They were a company that had shoe shops worldwide. The jobs on offer were as sales managers mainly in Africa. They had shops in England. As I pointed out in the interview the shoes were not of the highest quality. The interviewer replied that not everyone could afford high quality shoes. I was offered a job.

The other areas that I was encouraged to explore were banking and insurance. There were opportunities with the domestic banks, but they did not appeal to me. There was, however, also a company called Barclays DCI, which had an overseas banking network, and which appeared to have had many jobs. My friend, Cyril Woodberry, went to work for them. With hindsight, Barclays DCI had more to offer me than most of the other avenues which I pursued, but for some reason I never applied.

The father of my friend, Godfrey Shaw, worked for an Insurance Company in Manchester. Through him, I went for an interview. I was offered a job, but they did not have a graduate recruitment scheme and the salary on offer was only £450 per annum, whereas the "going rate" was between £700 and £750. Nevertheless the offer was there.

Returning to my interview with Mr Holloway, after I had rejected the Home Civil Service, he said: *What about the Foreign Office?* I replied that I would like that, but they wouldn't want people like me. To which he retorted: *You'll never know, if you don't apply!* Accordingly, I sent off for the application forms for the Foreign Office. When the forms arrived a few days later – there was no email, but the post was efficient in those days – the same application form was used for:

The Foreign Office Administrative Class
The Foreign Office Executive Class
The Home Civil Service Administrative Class
The Home Civil Service Executive Class; and
The Special Departmental Class.

I decided to tick the boxes to apply for them all. I was already qualified for the two Executive Class competitions by virtue of my A Level results. I did not get a positive response from the Foreign Office, but I did from the Home Civil Service. I was invited to go to Manchester Airport at Ringway to talk to the Immigration Officers there. At that time Ringway was quite a small airport, but it was sufficiently big to employ three or four Immigration Officers. A number of people, including my doctor in Wymeswold, had suggested to me that employment as an Immigration Officer would be a good way of using my language skills. The chaps who interviewed me were a lively bunch and clearly enjoyed their work. They also pointed out that the irregular hours brought additional financial rewards. By 1962 immigration had already become a burning political issue in the UK and indeed had culminated in the Commonwealth Immigrants Act enacted in April 1962. So the job of Immigration Officers was to stop foreigners coming in, whereas, having spent 18 months or so in France, my inclinations were to allow as much free movement as possible. Whether explicitly or implicitly, I no doubt transmitted my unease to my hosts. Sometime later, I received a letter to say that I had been allocated to the Ministry of Power.

I also had an interview with a man – a very nice man! – from an organisation which I had never heard of before, called GCHQ, which was based in Cheltenham. These letters stand for Government Communications Headquarters. He told me that the work involved was secret and he could not tell me much more unless I was really interested. I told him I was not. Nevertheless he encouraged me to pursue my interest in the Foreign Office.

The paths of the two administrative class and the special departmental class competitions were the same: interviews in London, plus an Oxbridge type honours degree level examination in one's chosen subject, in my case French. The interviews and the examination papers were to be given a mark; places were to be allocated on the basis of the total marks received. Thus, for example, if there were 10 posts available in the Foreign Office, they would be offered to the 10 people with the most marks who had applied to the Foreign Office.

I went for an interview for the Administrative Class. This was a very daunting affair. I was ushered into a large room where about ten distinguished-looking middle-aged men were sitting round an enormous semi-circle of polished wooden tables. I think I acquitted myself reasonably well, apart from making an enormous *faux-pas*. I heard myself saying at one point that I thought patriotism was dead. Though I tried to wriggle out of it by saying that, of course we should put Britain first, the panel returned to the charge on a number of occasions.

I also went for an interview for the Special Departmental Class. This was designed to recruit potential managers for three Government bodies which had large regional organisations: the Post Office, the Inland Revenue and the Ministry of Labour. On the application form I put the three departments in that order of preference. In those days, the train journey from Manchester to London took many hours. On the way down, I reflected that I would prefer the Post Office, but I would prefer to be dealing with people in the Ministry of Labour, rather than taxes in the Inland Revenue. I will never know whether that was the right decision! The interview was much more informal – only one man from each of the three departments, plus one from the Civil Service Commission. I think they were quite amused to ask me why I had changed my mind, though the man from the tax office was possibly a little miffed that I had rejected what most would have regarded as a more prestigious position.

I sat the written examination in Manchester ten days or so after I had finished my finals. There were seven written papers for the Administrative Class, but candidates had to choose only five to count for the Special Departmental Class. There were the usual translation and essay papers, plus examinations in Poetry, the Novel and Drama and one on Mediaeval Literature. As was the tradition in Oxford and Cambridge there were no set books for any of these examinations.

I dropped Mediaeval Literature and one other from my Special Departmental Class choices. It was not long before I realised that had been a mistake, because, although I didn't think I was particularly good at it, I probably had a comparative advantage. Manchester was one of the top universities for mediaeval French literature, so I was better placed than most to deal with any questions that were asked.

I don't remember anything about the examinations apart from one question on the poetry paper. When I came to choose the final question to answer, there were none left on any poet whom I had studied. So I decided to answer the question about Paul Valéry. I knew half a line of his poetry: *Un creux toujours futur*. I spent the next three-quarters of an hour comparing him to Mallarmé!

I received the results of my endeavours by post in Belley in the middle of August. I did not have enough marks to qualify for the Administrative Class. I did not have enough marks to qualify for the Post Office. But I did have enough marks for the Ministry of Labour and the Inland Revenue. As I had chosen the Ministry of Labour, I was offered a post there at an annual salary of £709 (compared with £750 in the Administrative Class). I have written about what happened there in my next book *Adventures of a Civil Servant*.

The Final Fling

I arranged with the CCCS to go back to Belley for a final session as *moniteur* in a *colonie de vacances*. I decided to hitch-hike there. I had only been to Germany once and I had never been to Belgium. So I devised a route through Belgium and Germany. There were few motorways at that time outside Germany and Italy, so my route took me along the national roads from Ostend, through Bruges, Ghent, Brussels, Louvain, and Liège to Aachen in Germany. It was a hot July day, when I saw Brussels for the first time. Later on I went through the Neckar valley through Calw and on to Rottweil, where I spent the night and which I liked very much. Then on into Switzerland and eventually to Belley.

It was late July. Paulette and Robert were there with their two boys. Monique was also there. I immediately started pestering Monique, but without success.

The new director and his wife arrived a couple of days later along with the new team of *moniteurs* and *monitrices*. Among them was an eighteen year-old girl, called Anne-Marie. I immediately turned my attentions to her with rather more success. We got on well together. In particular, we hitch-hiked to Geneva on one of our days off. It was a hot August day and Anne-Marie wanted to bathe in Lake Geneva, which she did. She persuaded me to go in too. I did, but only stayed in a few seconds. The water, which had come down from the Alps was icy cold, even in August.

Me and my team, Belley, August 1962[5]

Towards the end of our stay, the CCCS were asking for volunteers to do the washing-up at a centre somewhere in Switzerland. Anne-Marie and I volunteered, but her parents said "no". It was probably a wise move on their part, and, as in those days she was still a minor, she had to comply.

We did, however, arrange to meet again in Besançon at the beginning of September. Claude Talon and Mady were married by this time. Mady's parents had a large villa in Besançon which was unoccupied most of the time. Claude said I could stay there "provided that I didn't bring any girls into the house". Anne-Marie came to Besançon for a few days and stayed with her friend … Floriane! (Anne-Marie also knew Denise Tessier and Eliane who had been with me at Anglet two years' before.)

---

[5] I had originally included this in the chapter on Belley in July 1961. Then I noticed that I am wearing the pullover which I bought at Plouha in August 1961!

After that I went to Darney in the Vosges and spent a few days with Paulette and Robert. At that time they lived in an old house in the village, in accommodation provided by virtue of Paulette's employment as a school-mistress. Robert was a forest warden employed by the Government. He was responsible for the well-being of a section of the local beech forest. He took me out to the forest one day. Different parts of the forest were at different stages of development. At one end of the spectrum there was a clearing. All but one of the trees in this area had been felled. The one 150-year old tree, dating from the time of Napoleon, had been selected, because of its good health, to survive for another 150 years. The idea was that it would drop its seeds in the clearing and some of these would germinate and grow into new trees. Another section of the forest contained a large number of young trees, which had grown in an earlier clearing. Most of these would soon be thinned out so that the strongest-looking ones would have enough space to develop. Other sections of the forest were at further stages of development or maturity. The final section of forest consisted of trees that were ready for "harvesting" – the economic justification for the whole process! But one of these 150-year-old trees would be spared to survive for another 150 years. Robert had to decide which one!

Epilogue

Some sixty years later, I am still in touch with many of the people whom I met during this period. From Manchester, we see Godfrey Shaw and his wife, Beryl, regularly, mostly at their home in Great Missenden, where they have been kind hosts, before and after our stays in Antibes. They have also been out to stay with us in Antibes a few times and twice ventured into the wilds of Lincolnshire. I exchange Christmas greetings with Roy Reader, though I have only seen him once (in the 1980s) since our wedding in 1965. I have recently re-established contact with Bryn James, who was a teacher in Knutsford until his retirement. I met Cyril Woodberry and John Jordan at Beryl and Godfrey's. John Jordan spent the whole of his working life as a teacher at Leeds Grammar School. He sadly passed away a few years ago. I was also in touch with Bob Davies and he came to our house in Birmingham in the sixties, but he died when he was about forty.

Cyril joined Barclays DCO. He lived in Coseley in the Black Country. In the course of 1963 I went to a dance in Wolverhampton and bumped into Cyril. He invited me to go to visit him at his house in Coseley. I arranged to go a few weeks later. I got a bus from Walsall, where I was living at the time, to Wednesbury. From there I needed to get a bus to Coseley. I was wandering around the bus station, but couldn't find what I was looking for. Eventually I stopped a man and asked politely: "Can you tell me where I can get a bus to Coseley, please?" (I pronounced 'bus' with an 's' and Coseley with a 'z'.) The man looked puzzled for a moment. Then he said: "Oah, yer want a buzz to Coassly, do yer?"

I have met and stayed with many of the friends I met in France during this period, both on my own and with my family. In particular, we have stayed with Paulette and Robert. They moved soon after I knew them to a new modern villa on the outskirts of Darney. Their address was still very short: Cuny, 88 Darney, France! In the summer of 1978, we stayed with them on the way back from camping in Germany. We had had to put our tent away wet, so we erected it again in their garden to dry. This was not, however, a very happy stay, as they were mourning the death of their nineteen year-old niece, who had been murdered recently, while hitch-hiking. One day in the eighties, I went (on my own from Strasbourg) to see them. There had been a hurricane a few weeks before: vast swathes of the forest had been completely flattened. Paulette said she had been in the house on her own and she had been terrified: there had been hailstones the size of golf balls; she showed me the dents they had made in the ornamental zinc sheet on the front of the house. In his early days, Robert drove a Panhard car, which was one of a number of slightly eccentric French cars that were around at that time. The last time we went to stay with them, they had a Mercedes. They arranged for us all to meet Robert's sister and her husband at a restaurant. There was some confusion about the arrangements and the other couple were late. When they arrived the brother-in-law said that he had been asking if anyone had seen some peasants in a Mercedes! They came to stay with us in Brussels in the nineties. One evening we took them to a very popular restaurant in the centre of Brussels, called *Chez Léon*. It was a large restaurant, which had been created by joining together a number of old houses. It was a rabbit-warren of corridors, steps, crooked staircases and uneven floors. The restaurant specialised in beef steak and *moules*. We had one of two tables, in an alcove at the top of a short flight of three or four steps. The youngish couple at the other table, who were also French, ordered *moules*. When the waiter arrived with the large bowl of steaming hot *moules* in a very liquid *marinière* sauce, he tripped on the stairs and threw the contents of his bowl all over the back of Robert and the front of the younger couple. Fortunately, no-one was hurt, but it didn't do their clothes, or Robert's temper, much good. I kept in touch with them until they were both in their nineties. I never knew their full postal address. Unfortunately a couple of years ago, my New Year's card was returned to me 'Address unknown'.

We visited the Queneys on many occasions. In particular, we went to stay with them at Péage de Roussillon on the banks of the Rhône in May 1973 and were there for our son Jon's third birthday. They had both obtained teaching posts there. Thursday was still the traditional day off. They asked where we wanted to go. We said "not too far". So we got in their Peugeot 504 and set off southwards. We stopped at Avignon and danced on the bridge (or not, as the case may be – Jon refused). I was put in charge of navigation and we took a wrong turning. Finally we had a picnic on the banks of the Rhône, somewhere south of Arles. Eventually, at about four o'clock in the afternoon we arrived at Saintes Maries de la Mer on the Mediterranean, some 300 kilometres from where we started out. I had just sat down in a café with a drink – a *Perrier citron* – when Andrée said, it was time to start our journey back. We called in at Nimes and visited the Roman amphitheatre. Then we went to the Alpilles and visited the windmill made famous by Alphonse Daudet. I took a photo in the golden evening sunlight. I had it framed and I still have it on my office wall, which I can see – somewhat faded – when I look up from my computer, as I am typing this. On the Saturday, Marcel took us to a small vineyard at Tavel. He took some jerry cans with him. These were filled up by means of the same sort of device as is used for putting petrol in the car. I noted that a litre of wine was cheaper than a litre of petrol.

They both managed to get transferred back to Besançon and had a new house built on a hill just outside the city at Montfaucon. It had a large picture window with a magnificent panoramic view over the undulating countryside. When I first met him, Marcel was an old man at forty years of age. The war had left its mark. One time when we went to visit them in Besançon, having not seen them for several years and Marcel would have been nearly sixty, I said to Jennifer: "Marcel will not have changed". He hadn't.

Nor had he changed the last time we saw him – in 1993. By that time he would have been in his mid-seventies, but he still had the same boyish grin. We stayed in a discrete apartment in one of their properties at Malbuisson. Unfortunately by this time their son, Jean-François had died, but we met their three granddaughters, including the delightful and appropriately named Mélusine, who was about five years old at that time.

While we were staying there, we decided to drive to Montreux, which, as I have already said, my grandmother described as the most beautiful place in the world. When I worked at the UK Representation in Brussels, I became quite friendly with an Italian Diplomat, whose name was Francesco di Medici. He had previously been Italian Consul in the east of Switzerland. He did not like the Swiss, whom he described as "a nation of policemen". We were driving along the main street of Montreux, which had tram lines running along one side of it. I had gone further than I should have, before I saw the underground carpark that I was looking for. I turned sharp right across the tram lines to go into the carpark, conscious of the fact that I may well have performed an illegal manoeuvre. I parked the car at midday and Jennifer and I walked along the side of the lake. It was a beautiful day and we had lunch outside at a restaurant by the lake. After a lazy afternoon, we arrived back at the carpark at six p.m. We paid for our car parking ticket and returned to the car, only to find that it had been … clamped! There was a notice on the car telling us to report to the local police station. I was furious. I jumped to the conclusion that this had something to do with my illegal manoeuvre and vowed never to go to Switzerland again. Jennifer, on the other hand, was quietly amused. We eventually found the police station and were kept waiting for twenty minutes or so. Then two policemen came out and looked at us. Without addressing us directly, one said to the other: "It's not them, they're too old!" Jennifer was 49 at the time! Finally we were taken into the inner office. Some questions were put to us as a formality, but they weren't really interested in us anymore. I asked why our car had been clamped and they said they were looking for some drug dealers who had a red car with a Belgian registration plate. I was greatly relieved that I was not going to be charged with an offence and by then mildly amused at the whole incident. Jennifer, on the other hand, was furious at the incompetence and waste of our time.

Both Marcel and Andrée died some years later. Other people that I kept in touch with until they died were Charles Baudard, André Proudhon and Louis Garret.

Charles' and André's colleague, Maurice Moyse, is 98 years old and still going strong at the time of writing (2020). We went to see him at his apartment in Besançon in 2012, just after his ninetieth birthday and, we learned, shortly after his wife had died. We made the arrangements for the visit by email. He invited us for lunch *en toute simplicité*. We had his phone number, but he told me not to ring, as he was very deaf. He greeted us and ushered us into a large living/dining room. He was as alert and charming as ever. He picked up a notepad and pencil and handed it to me explaining that he could talk, but I would need to write my answers down on the notepad. It worked! He opened a bottle of champagne and invited us to partake of an aperitif, with appropriate nibbles. His daughter joined us. A little later we sat down for a three- (or four-) course meal, including roast lamb. He had prepared everything, apart from the dessert, which his daughter had brought.

After lunch we were invited to go back to our hotel for a rest. I think the rest lasted about a quarter of an hour. Then he offered to take us for a walk round the city, which I had hardly visited for 50 years. He reminded me of things that I had once known and showed me things that I had never seen before. He had some business to attend to (bank or Post Office) so he left us to rest in a café while he attended to his business.

After all this time, we got on very well together. On the spur of the moment his daughter invited us to her house for an evening aperitif. Accordingly, we spent a very pleasant early evening chatting in her garden.

I kept in touch with Louis Garret for many years. He eventually obtained his CAPES and got a teaching post in Vesoul, where I visited him and his wife on a number of occasions. Before he was married, he came to stay with us in

Walsall. It was July 1966. England played West Germany in the football World Cup Final on the Saturday, while he was there. We didn't have a television, but I had asked the owner of our flat, who lived on the ground floor, if we could watch the match on her television – the only time I ever made such a request. She agreed. I asked Louis if he wanted to watch the match. He said that he was not interested in football. To my credit – and utter amazement ever since – I said no more about it. We got on a bus and went to a local beauty spot, Barr Beacon. Normally on a sunny July Saturday the place would be crowded. That day it was practically deserted. I took Jennifer's little red transistor radio with me, but refrained from switching it on until we got to the bus stop to return to Walsall. It was just coming up to full time and England were winning 2-1. As I got on the bus, Germany scored, so the match was going into extra time. It would take about 20 minutes for us to get back to our flat in Walsall, so I thought we would get back in time for me to watch the last ten minutes. As we were hurrying to get back to the flat, we passed a flower shop – about three minutes from home. Louis decided that he wanted to buy Jennifer some flowers to thank her for her hospitality. After some considerable time-consuming deliberation he bought her some roses. Jennifer says it is the only time a young man ever bought her a bunch of red roses. The match was over by the time we got back into the flat. At least England won!

    I have already mentioned that we have met Paulette Boissard, Gérard Althuser, Jean-Claude Boutonnet and Claude Talon on many occasions, so I will not repeat myself. I have recently had Skype conversations with Paulette and my U3A French group!

****

This was meant to be the story of my bike. In fact the significance of the bike fizzled out after I left Besançon and has not been mentioned since the early autumn of 1961. Nevertheless my sons will tell you that when we were travelling in parts of the East Midlands in England, in eastern France or Switzerland I would say to them: "I went there on my bike!"

APPENDIX

Saint-Exupéry and the Meaning of Human Existence

B.A. Thesis presented by

J.W. MACKLEY

1962

ANTOINE DE SAINT-EXUPÉRY

ŒUVRES

COURRIER SUD · VOL DE NUIT
TERRE DES HOMMES · PILOTE DE GUERRE
LETTRE A UN OTAGE
LE PETIT PRINCE, illustré par l'auteur
CITADELLE

PRÉFACE DE ROGER CAILLOIS

BIBLIOTHÈQUE nrf DE LA PLÉIADE

Saint-Exupéry and the Meaning of Human Existence

Contents

Introduction	145
Chapter One Courrier Sud : The Initial Conflict of Ideals	148
Chapter Two Vol De Nuit : A Solution "In Miniature"	159
Chapter Three Terre Des Hommes : The First Universal Solution	168
Chapter Four Pilote De Guerre : The Shattering Of An Ideal And The Birth Of A Permanent One	176
Conclusion	186
Bibliographical Note	191

INTRODUCTION

It has become banal to say that the scientific advances of the twentieth century have brought about a tremendous upheaval of the values that were previously unchallenged. It is none the less true. No-where is this more true than in France, with its sensitivity to the vacillations of the Western world's conscience. The writers of France reflect this growing attitude of rejection of traditional values. From the initial rebellion of Baudelaire, to the near-nihilism of Valéry and the existentialism of J-P Sartre the agony is ever increasing. The question remains the same: What is the meaning of human existence?

Pierre-Henri Simon[1] suggests that for the first thirty years of the century they all found their solution in a basically humanist creed. With *Les Conquérants* by Malraux a new note is struck. There can be no finite solution to the problem of human existence.

The defeated characters, for Malraux, are those like Tchen Dai, who think they have found a permanent solution to this problem. To be a conqueror the hero must retain his lucidity and maintain at the same time the tension of knowing that life has no transcendental values. There is no such thing as humanism for Garine, the hero of *Les Conquérants*.

> *Je n'aime pas les hommes*

he confesses early in the novel.[2] The only value, the only reason for living is to be found in the tragic awareness of the individual of the futility of his own existence. This Monsieur Simon calls:

> *l'angoisse de s'éprouver contingent et mortel*

---

[1] L'Homme en Procès pp. 8–10.
[2] p. 68 (Livre de Poche) *Les Conquérants*.

There is a tendency, he says, for the authors to emphasize the physical and sensual aspects of their existence. Of these at least they are sure, though their duration is limited.

Yet however dark the gloom of *La Voie Royale* where man is fighting a losing battle against Death, the hero, Perken, is trying to transcend his contingency:

Je voudrais laisser une cicatrice sur cette carte

This is the first, almost barbaric, conception of the search for eternity which characterizes the new hero.

"Hero" indeed seems to have become the operative word. For Antoine de Saint-Exupéry, born a year before Malraux, in 1900, the notion of the hero is equally present. The thought of the two writers seems to have undergone largely similar influences. Both are indebted to Pascal for their awareness of the misery of the human condition, both borrow from Nietzsche the urge to find an individual transcendental solution to the problem of human existence.

The early Malraux was a turbulent figure, an adventurer. His outlook was profoundly pessimistic. The personal conflict was of a very lucid nature: he was tragically aware of the absurdity of existence and yet he felt there was some way of finding a solution. In Saint-Exupéry the conflict tends to be subconscious. On the one hand he feels the world is meaningless, on the other hand he is sure it cannot be so.

In his childhood and youth Saint-Exupéry enjoyed a succession of stabilizing influences. In spite of frequent changes of abode his childhood, we gather, was extraordinarily happy. He acquired a love of nature, he valued friendship and above all he seems to have had that *joie de vivre* which French literature has preserved from the time of Villon and Rabelais right up to such modern writers as Colette and Giono, but which is noticeably lacking in Malraux and Sartre. Indeed, Saint-Exupéry's acquaintances are unanimous in indicating his warmth of personality and spontaneous, albeit somewhat shy, friendship. This warmth of personality is typified in one of his own works, *Lettre à un Otage* where he emphasizes the value of *le sourire* and where he remembers, with sincere depth of feeling, a pre-war *Pernod* he had shared with friends at Tournus on the banks of the Saône.

The joys of simple human relationships alone, it would seem, could not be sufficient to give life a meaning. Saint-Exupéry follows in the steps of Virgil and the Roman poets in wanting his life to achieve some sort of eternity by giving to it something which would give it a value after death. He could never accept work as merely a means of making a livelihood. It had, in addition, to fulfil two conditions: it had to have some intrinsic elevating value and it had to have a use. It had to serve in the material and moral advancement of man. Thus when he was forced for a time to accept an earthbound job, he had an inner compulsion to go back to flying, to escape from this apparently fruitless existence.

Saint-Exupéry's temperament, it would seem, contains two tendencies which are diametrically opposed: the love of simple human relationships and the desire to escape from their bounds. It would be an exaggeration to say that Saint-Exupéry's work consists entirely of an attempt to reconcile these two tendencies. There is however definitely a thread running through his work which attempts to put them into perspective. It is the progress of this thread which we shall try to follow in the coming pages. The question to be answered is: which (if either) of these two ways of life gives the true meaning to human existence and what is that meaning?

CHAPTER ONE
Courrier Sud: THE INITIAL CONFLICT OF IDEALS

Saint-Exupéry's first attempt at novel-writing is *Courrier Sud*. He published the work in 1928, that is to say when he was still working for the *Société d'Aviation Latécoère*, the company which forms the background to the action of *Courrier Sud*. Briefly this work consists of the meditations of a young man called Jacques Bernis flying on the Toulouse-Dakar air-route. He is in search of a meaning to his existence. As he flies he reflects upon the two worlds which two months previously had seemed open to him: the world of the hero and the world of simple human relationships.

The author takes us back in time to tell us of the attraction that the simple world of human love had had for Bernis. This world is symbolized by a woman called Geneviève whom he had known when she was fifteen, who had since married and had one son. During his last leave which he had spent in Paris, he had revisited Geneviève. His relationship with her from childhood to manhood is described and from these details we obtain a reasonable picture of why the ultimate solution was not satisfactory.

The world to which Bernis returns after two years' absence is a world of tradition, a world of simple human responsibilities. In Part Two, Chapter One of *Courrier Sud* we read:

> *Tous étaient prisonniers d'eux-mêmes, limités par ce frein obscure et non comme lui, ce fugitive, cet enfant pauvre, ce magicien*[3]

This world was not a changing world. It had never formed a part of progressive modern society. It was a world which

---
[3] p. 16.

evolved very slowly in the natural process of Darwinian evolution, a world beaten into shape by time and habits:

> *Dans le monde le plus immuable où, pour toucher un mur, pour allonger un champ, il fallait vingt ans de procès.*[4]

Geneviève belonged inextricably to this world even as a child. The author romanticizes it so that Geneviève is portrayed like a fairy living among the trees so essential to this almost mythical world of Nature to which she belongs, that she becomes identified with it.

> *Tu nous paraissais éternelle d'être si bien liée aux choses, si sûre des choses, de tes pensées, de ton avenir.*[5]

We have seen the first mention of eternity, with reference to Geneviève. It seems here to be only apparent eternity. It was the eternity of this young girl that was to capture their hearts. This is the eternity of the simple life:

> *Dans ton royaume une saison apporte les fleurs, l'automne les fruits, une saison apporte l'amour : la vie est simple.*[6]

Bernis' hope in loving Geneviève was to have a taste of the happiness which he knew she enjoyed. If we examine the nature of her happiness we realize immediately why Bernis could never share it.

Her happiness is closely linked with her intuitive sense of eternity. This eternity resembles the Buddhist conception of Nirvana, which is the state of beatitude resulting from the extinction of individuality.[7] Even though as a child Geneviève

---

[4] p. 17.
[5] p. 20.
[6] p. 21.
[7] Concise Oxford Dictionary.

has not reached this state, she no longer exists as a detached individual. She is a sort of princess in the world of Nature in which she moved, closely bound to it and as nothing without it.

When she becomes a mother we can expect full integration into her compact little world, whose meaning is in the continuation of existence. These expectations are fulfilled and we see Geneviève bathed in the sacred mystery of her life like a simple priestess bathed in the mystery of her religion. When her son is born she becomes quite certain of this world.

> *Une évidence plus forte que les autres. Elle avait servi cet enfant à la surface des choses et parmi d'autres choses vivantes (…) Elle s'était sentie … mais oui, c'est cela : intelligente. Et sûre d'elle-même et liée à tout et faisant partie d'un grand concert*[8]

This conception of existence is perhaps based on intuition rather than reason and it is certain that Bernis would not be able to accept its passive nature. Nevertheless its value for so many women including Geneviève would not be diminished on that account. It is a world in which the natural procreation of Life is the prime object. As the men and women, the animals and plants, engaged in this process are working together towards the same ends they achieve a sort of pantheistic unity. In their unity they tend to lose their identity until they come together to form a concordant body of simple, joyful, satisfied life working together in making Life eternal. This then is a world with its foundations in an intuitive sense of security and belonging, rather than in rationalistic principles, but the mystic harmony between Geneviève and this world seems to be sufficient

---

[8] p. 27. This interpretation seems to me more plausible than Luc Estang's suggestion (p. 126. *Saint-Exupéry par lui-même*) that Geneviève feels a visceral attachment to the world through the child that had been born to her.

evidence for accepting its validity. As we shall see it is not valid for everyone, but for Geneviève (and later we shall see, for Simone Fabien)[9] it is the only valid existence.

Thus we have for the first time in the works of Saint-Exupéry a notion of the eternity of life, though here eternity must mean going beyond the bounds of individual existence rather than "infinite" or "immortal" existence. In this eternity the individual becomes part of life which, in 1928 when the work was written, had been going on, perhaps improving and certainly increasing its strength, for a very long time, and which had every prospect of doing so for an immeasurable time in the future. So the individual becomes confused not only with its own surroundings but with life in general.

In direct contrast to this world of simple love we get a glimpse of the utopia for which Jacques Bernis is striving. Bernis was a childhood friend of the narrator, and it is largely by means of light thrown on his character by the narrator's own reminiscences that we find the cause of Bernis' search for a utopia beyond the traditional values he has been taught as a child to cherish. As children[10] they had been convinced that beyond the *tumulte vain de la surface* in which their parents had lived, that is to say, beyond the parts of the house and grounds where people normally went, lay hidden mysteries and a hidden material treasure

> *exactement décrit dans les contes de fées : saphirs, opales, diamants.*

In this childhood they had therefore an insuperable desire to get to know *l'envers des choses*. As the author twice remarks they cannot find the whole truth if they remain tied up in this evolutionary cycle:

---

[9] c.f. *Vol de Nuit*.
[10] Part III, Chapter 3, pp. 60–63.

Fuir, voilà l'important[11]

It should come as no surprise to us to find that when he grows up and becomes a pilot, Jacques Bernis strives towards a utopia with values developed from this childhood dream. From a letter he sent to his friend, the narrator, we can deduce the main values of the world he is trying to attain.

From the whole tone of the letter we have the impression that Bernis is obsessed with the idea of novelty, the opposite pole to the idea of routine which most careers entail. This is revealed as he recalls the exciting experiences of his first flight over Spain to Tangiers. On this flight he had experienced new sensations which he would remember for ever, but which, alas, would soon become ordinary. He had discovered new towns from an angle which few people had seen before. He had discovered new people.

In spite of Chevrier's view that the pilot had a strong emotional attachment to the earth[12] the following passage would suggest that he was not satisfied with his discoveries but had to carry on to find new lands, new sensations:

> *Et puis, tu me connais, cette hâte de repartir, de chercher plus loin ce que je pressentais et ne comprenais pas, car j'étais ce sourcier dont le coudrier tremble et qu'il promène sur le monde jusqu'au trésor.*[13]

If we examine the routes of this pleasure and the desire to renew it elsewhere, we might possibly discover in the pilot's motives a desire for the omniscience of the Godhead, an insatiable desire, similar to that of the Humanists of the early Renaissance period,

---

[11] p. 61.
[12] Chevrier, p.48.
[13] p. 18.

to have a superficial acquaintance with every human experience. The difference, of course, is that their desire was intellectual while Bernis' desire was emotional.

Much more important than the initial pleasures he obtained from his *métier* no matter what interpretation we give to them, is the goal at which he seems to be aiming. We see clearly that he has been aiming to find the secret behind human existence. This he expresses in despairing terms, because he has begun to presume that there would be no absolute and unique solution. Its sense is nevertheless clear:

> *Pourquoi, pour la première fois, je ne découvre pas de source et me sens si loin du trésor ?*

Up to that time it seems that the new experiences he has undergone had been sufficient to provide for Bernis a taste of the treasure for which he has been searching. He was soon to realize that the more ardent his search, the more inaccessible this 'treasure' which would give a meaning to his existence,[14] was to become. He turned his attention, inwards, homewards, and decided that the inspiration he needed was to be found in Geneviève. This of course proved to be an illusion so that after the Genevieve episode, he had still not discovered his solution.

However the letter to the narrator[15] seems to give us the clue to what he is searching for. We see something which is at the same time a *source* and a *trésor,* the one is the beginning of the conquest, the other, the end. Surely the search for something which combines the two elements can be a search for only one

---

[14] Luc Estang also suggests that the 'treasure' was something rather than somewhere: "Ce n'est peut-être pas d'arriver quelque part qui lui importe mais de trouver quelque chose" (*Saint-Exupéry par lui-même,* p. 48.)
[15] pp. 17, 18, 21, 22.

thing that is the Supreme Truth of Life, the One, the Godhead, the immortal inspiration. The desire of Bernis, therefore, is to transcend the bounds of the human estate to become a sort of superman.

It would be impossible for him to accept the values of a limited society, for he had an insatiable urge to get beyond things he already knew, a secret driving force, an *Urgeist* as Goethe calls it, compelling him on

> *dans ce fond des mers où nous appelait notre inquiétude.*[16]

There can be no better way of summing up Bernis' character than using the author's own obituary of his friend by quoting two of his *confessions*

> *J'ai aimé une vie que je n'ai pas très bien comprise, une vie pas tout à fait fidèle. Je ne sais pas très bien ce dont j'ai eu besoin : c'était une fringale légère…*[17]

> *Ce que je devinais se cachait derrière toute chose. Il me semblait qu'avec un effort j'allais comprendre, j'allais le connaitre enfin et l'emporter. Et je m'en vais troublé par cette présence d'ami que je n'ai jamais pu tirer au jour…*[18]

And symbolically the narrator suggests that it was in trying to reach the highest of all the stars that Bernis met his death. Saint-Exupéry has realized that Man cannot reach perfection and Truth so easily:

> *Dans l'étoile la plus verticale a lui le trésor ô fugitif !*[19]

---

[16] p. 21.
[17] p. 76.
[18] pp. 76–77.
[19] p. 77.

It is not difficult for us to realize that the worlds of Geneviève and Bernis were poles apart and therefore quite incompatible. The simple community of Geneviève was founded on the acceptance by its members that that community is the world best suited to their existence, a haven sheltered from the dangerous and treacherous seas of adventure which offered no temptation to their earth-bound minds. Geneviève lived in her *royaume*; Bernis and the younger narrator tried to drag her to their other world, but as the narrator points out Geneviève is alive in her own environment. To change her environment would be to change Geneviève

> *Et Geneviève, emportée par toi, sera privée de Geneviève.*[20]

This indeed proves to be true. Bernis does not make a decision to return from their elopement:

> *Cette décision, pensait Bernis, cette décision a été prise en dehors de nous.*[21]

Bernis is therefore the romantic character whose unhappiness lies in his loneliness in a sympathetic environment. Each society is ready to accept him: Genevieve, the worlds of the spiritual[22] and carnal love,[23] the world of the narrator, all seem to woo him and he sees how for other people these lives have a meaning. Even the world of action does not provide the meaning he is looking for. The question of the narrator:

> *Où vas-tu maintenant chercher le trésor… ?*[24]

---

[20] p. 33.
[21] p. 42.
[22] Part II, Chapter XI, .pp. 44–47.
[23] Part II, Chapter XII, XIII, XIV, pp. 47–51.
[24] p. 68.

remains unanswered for Bernis. For him there are no limits and there is no end to his search and so it can never bear fruit.

The narrator does not propose a full solution to the problem, but he suggests in the same paragraph that one must recognise the limitations of one's existence:

> *Ce désert sur lequel je marche, moi qui suis retenu comme un plomb, au sol, je n'y saurais rien découvrir…*

… and he seems to suggest that he would not want to look for anything …

> *… Mais il n'est pour toi, magicien, qu'un voile de sable, qu'une apparence*[25]

After this episode Bernis is about to find a last escape from the world of reality by landing in the middle of the desert into a strange fairy-land of wonderment where he meets the isolated sergeant.

Bernis is therefore in many ways an outsider to full human relationships. By trying to enjoy all kinds of existence, by trying to form a delicate balance between one and another he achieves nothing but disillusionment. There are several alternatives open to a man and he has to choose. Once the choice is made he has to plunge himself into that life with all that he has and by this sacrifice, by accepting the limitations, he reaps the harvest.

This solution which is developed more fully in *Pilote de Guerre* is only suggested in *Courrier Sud* as Bernis never really sees the choice – he sees love and marriage as a complement to his life, not as a different life.

The narrator on the other hand has made his choice. By his example we have some idea of the solution that he would

---

[25] p. 68.

advocate for Bernis. We saw above that he had accepted his limitations. He had escaped from the world of Geneviève but he had accepted another similar world, though one with more conscious ideals and limitations than was the case in the intuitive world of Geneviève.

We see his approval of her world, or at least his acceptance of it in his letter to Bernis:

> *Je crois…la vie s'appuie sur autre chose…Ces coutumes, ces conventions, ces lois, tout ce dont tu ne sens pas la nécessité, tout ce dont tu t'es évadé…C'est cela qui lui donne un cadre…*[26]

Thus the character of the narrator shows no internal conflict. He has arrived at the compromise which satisfies him, but which Sartre might describe as being "in bad faith": he has left the mediocrity of the closed society to find a new existence which is practically earth-bound and whose limitations and finality he has accepted.

He seems satisfied with the life at Cap Juby though he gives little indication of the precise nature of the satisfactions which this existence gave him.

From his personal appearance towards the end of the work, we can assume that his work had a very active decisive nature which might have given it qualities which Rivière, the central character of Saint-Exupéry's next work *Vol de Nuit*, might have admired, though his character has a very definite poetic streak which makes him in some ways close to Bernis himself. He seems however to accept his position with dignity and enthusiasm as witnessed by his efficiency in carrying out the operation searching for Bernis.

---

[26] p. 33.

There seems to be little that is transcendental about this life, though there are surely early seeds of *Terre des Hommes* in the author's incidental remark during Bernis' last flight:

> *les camarades nous ont tiré de là. Et si nous étions faibles, nous ont hissés dans la carlingue : poignet de fer des camarades qui nous tiraient hors de ce monde dans leur monde.*[27]

---

[27] p. 69.

CHAPTER TWO
Vol de Nuit : A SOLUTION "IN MINATURE"

In the three years that have elapsed between the publication of *Courrier Sud* and that of his next novel, *Vol de Nuit*, published in 1931, Saint-Exupéry's thought seems to have crystallized and become more sure. In the first chapter the temptation of the world typified by Geneviève is set out in some detail, only to be regretted by the pilot:

> *ce village défendait, par sa seule immobilité, le secret de ses passions, ce village refusait sa douceur : il eût fallu renoncer à l'action pour la conquérir.*[28]

In this sentence we also see what is going to be the keynote of the novel: *l'action*. Action is going to be the inspiration for the heroes of *Vol de Nuit*. It might even seem that Bernis has found the treasure for which he was searching. The author at least seems more sure of himself.

In *Vol de Nuit* we have the description by Saint-Exupéry, in novel form, of an ideal society in microcosm. The action centres on Buenos Aires, where Rivière, the head of the South American Postal network, is awaiting the arrival of his aeroplane flying in with the mail from Patagonia, Chile and Paraguay, in time to catch the plane which is due to fly to Europe. Rivière is, as it were, the God of this society and the ideas in the novel show the author's concern with the problem of running an ideal society based on more advanced precepts than those found in the society typified by Geneviève. As we see, when the unfortunate employee called Roblet is dismissed after a lifetime of service with the company because of one

---

[28] p. 82.

mistake,[29] it is an authoritative society. Rivière is the master and upon his decisions depends the happiness of his staff.

Rivière combines the "solid" elements of the narrator in *Courrier Sud* with the sense of grandeur and a need to go beyond the bounds of simple existence. In spite of his assured attitude he does have doubts, but he always overcomes them.

For Rivière life is a continual battle. He is the leader of an army fighting not against another army but against nature. The motivating force of his life is to be found in the sustained feeling of responsibility which he has when he is working. As we have just said this feeling is "sustained" and this word is perhaps the keynote of Riviera's character, for the meaning of life for him, as for so many of Malraux's heroes is to be found in the maintaining of a certain tension, which prevents the hero from lapsing into a living death:

> *Il n'y a pas d'arrivée définitive de tous les courriers*[30]

says Rivière in Chapter Two.

Rivière even more than Fabien, rejects the escape from tension that human love would offer him:

> *Il s'aperçut qu'il avait peu à peu repoussé vers la vieillesse, pour quand il aurait le temps ce qui fait douce la vie des hommes*[31]

Love would not have been an escape from the *métier*. Rivière did not need an escape: his life was full and had a definite meaning.

Not that he was without doubt about his existence. Indeed while they are waiting for news of Fabien, he is powerless before the arguments of Simone Fabien. But he does not give in. There is just no point of contact between her world and his world.

---

[29] pp. 105–106.
[30] p. 86.
[31] p. 85.

> *Cette femme parlait elle aussi au nom d'un monde absolu et des devoirs et de ses droite… Elle exigeait son bien et elle avait raison. Et lui aussi avait raison…*[32]

Thus logically there is no reason why he should prefer his world to hers. There is, however, a moral one:

> *Aimer, aimer seulement, quelle impasse*[33]

says Rivière. There must be more to life than this and he hits upon a phrase which he has read somewhere.

> *Il s'agit de les rendre éternels*

It is clear that Rivière is a man who recognizes the value of the world typified by Geneviève and now by Simone Fabien, but cannot find any personal reason to take refuge in this world. His world is not passive, but active: he needs to go beyond his mortality.

Rivière is a many-sided figure, but we have only space enough here to discuss this main ideal of eternity through action, and see how Rivière goes about achieving it through the people under him. To do this it is necessary to have a look at the world under his control.

The main characters of this world are, of course, the pilots. The administrators are concerned along with Rivière himself with the smooth functioning of the airmail company, that is to say, with extracting the maximum energy and efficiency from the pilots. Saint-Exupéry tells us very little about the pilots before they came to work for the company, but we can assume that they were quite ordinary, unpretentious, though quietly courageous,

---

[32] p. 120.
[33] p. 121.

young men. The pilot of the plane that is to go to Europe is described in Chapter Ten as

> *cet homme au milieu de ces millions d'hommes*

He would seem to be no one out of the ordinary and yet Rivière expects great things of him.

It is Rivière who must take most of the credit for the miracle he is to perform in transforming these men into the heroes they are to become. The strict discipline of Rivière seems to have been appreciated by the pilots, because it brought the required results; we learn in Rivière's own words what his aims were:

> *Il ne pensait pas les asservir par cette dureté, mais les lancer hors d'eux-mêmes*[34]

It will be interesting to see what new meaning will be given to the pilots' lives under the control of Rivière.

Even before the flight the pilot achieves a first limited ideal; he escapes beyond the bounds of routine. We see the description of the pilot's expectations from his journey in Chapter Ten. He is not an insignificant bureaucrat but carries a manly responsibility:

> *Elle (sa femme) regardait ces bras solides qui, dans une heure, porterait le sort du courrier d'Europe, responsables de quelque chose de grand, comme du sort d'une ville.*[35]

But in *Vol de Nuit* the feeling of responsibility is not overimportant as far as the pilots are concerned; it is Rivière who seems to make most of the decisions. However the pilots do have

---

[34] p. 92. Luc Estang puts forward a similar argument in quoting the following passage from the same paragraph.
"*Le règlement, pensait Rivière, est semblable aux rites d'une religion qui semblent absurdes, mais façonnent les hommes* » « *Façonner les hommes : le grand mot n'est-il pas lâché ? N'est-ce point la raison d'être de l'action ?* » (*Saint-Exupéry par lui-même*, p. 74.)
[35] p. 107.

to make decisions and when they do so, they can be important ones. In the first chapter Fabien says one word which is to have far reaching consequences. The word is *continuerons*[36]. The consequences include the wreckage of a plane, the loss of two men's lives, the loss of a cargo of mail, deep sorrow for a newly-married bride and a severe blow to Rivière's already hotly disputed plans. These, then, were all part of his responsibilities.

In any case the pilots can laugh at an existence bound up by routine and by the corresponding simple relationships which a regular life in a limited environment had to offer:

> *Elle (sa femme) le chargeait de tendre liens… mais à l'heure de chaque départ ces liens, sans qu'il en parût souffrir tombaient*[37]

Not that the security, which the town had to offer him, was likely to tempt him for very long. There was a sort of mutual distrust. He was not interested in the town and the town was not cut out to protect his safety, though for earthbound citizens it was a model of security:

> *Cette ville serrait les hommes dans ses cent mille forteresses ; tout était calme et sûr…cette ville endormie ne le protégeait pas : ses lumières lui sembleraient vaines, lorsqu'il se lèverait, jeune dieu, de leur poussière.*[38]

As for Bernis, flying represents an escape beyond the limited existence of an earthbound society. But the difference lies in the fact that the pilots of Rivière find a series of satisfying solutions to their desires. We see that in the action itself they have a first taste of the eternity for which Rivière has predestined them. This

---

[36] p. 82.
[37] p. 107.
[38] p. 107.

first taste did not come to all the pilots, but it came to Pellerin in his tremendous struggle with the elements over the Andes. The pilot of the plane bound for Europe also expected to renew the tension of life, to show that he was not "in bad faith" as Sartre would say, to show that he was aware of the intensity of the struggle for progress, the struggle to rise above the human estate and become a kind of superman:

> *Elle l'avait nourri, veillé et caressé, non pour elle-même, mais pour cette nuit qui allait le prendre. Pour des luttes, pour des angoisses, pour des victoires, dont elle ne connaîtrait rien.*[39]

We are not told of this pilot's struggles. We are told of Pellerin's. He is transported out of the world where mortal man is allowed to tread. He was flying in tranquillity over the *Cordillère des Andes* when suddenly he is caught up in a cyclone. But people have seen cyclones before and Pellerin remarks:

> *Le cyclone ce n'est rien. On sauve sa peau. Mais auparavant ! Mais cette rencontre que l'on fait !*[40]

We may ask ourselves what it was that he met. The answer seems to be a sort of pantheistic deity or perhaps simply a world of unreality, of mystery, the world of the supernatural. We are no longer in a world of physical objects, but in a world of moods. These moods were not human since there is no living soul within hundreds of miles. Pellerin describes the mood which seems to attack him as one of anger. Intuitively he sensed that it came from the natural objects that surrounded him:

> *A quoi devinait-il qu'elle (la colère) suintait des pierres, qu'elle suintait de la neige ?... Pellerin regardait, avec un serrement de cœur*

---

[39] p. 107.
[40] p. 89.

> *inexplicable, ces pics innocents, ces arêtes, ces crêtes de neige, à peine plus gris, et qui pourtant commençaient à vivre – comme un peuple.*[41]

There he was then in this fairyland to which his *métier* had brought him. He had had for a few seconds a glimpse of a supernatural world, but in the intensity of those few seconds he had engraved a new indelible experience on his memory.

We have seen earlier that Rivière aspired to a more lasting sense of eternity than this fleeting glimpse experienced by some of his pilots, when he said:

> *Il s'agit de les rendre éternels*[42]

Later however, he seems to contradict this thought by saying that he was not seeking for eternity, but for something else to protect man from the absurdity of existence:

> *…nous ne demandons pas à être éternels, mais à ne pas voir les actes et les choses tout à coup perdre leur sens. Le vide qui nous entoure se montre alors …*[43]

Paradoxically these two quotations seem to be complementary. Rivière is not seeking for individual eternity, but a collective immortality. In his doubt, which becomes quite anguished in Chapter XIV, Rivière asks why they are all acting as though there is something more important than human life:

> *…nous agissons toujours comme si quelque chose dépassait, en valeur, la vie humaine… Mais quoi ?*[44]

The answer for Rivière at any other time, would have been easy to find. Yet in his anguish it is some time before he

---

[41] p. 88.
[42] p. 121.
[43] p. 129.
[44] p. 120.

compares his action to that of a nomad chieftain who determined to show humanity that his race had existed.

> *Et il menait son peuple dresser au moins des pierres, que n'ensevelirait pas le désert.*[45]

The stones which Rivière found to put up in the desert consisted of the establishment of a regular night mail service. The lasting eternity which the pilots found was in the sense of belonging to a band of men dedicated to the furthering of human progress. Thus we have the birth of a sense of fraternity to which the author rarely refers in *Vol de Nuit* although we are told at least once of its presence, as if it were taken for granted. When the pilot from Asuncion is told of Fabien's death, the author makes this short comment:

> *Ils en parlèrent peu. Une grande fraternité les dispensait de phrases.*[46]

As Chevrier says:

> *Il (Rivière) veut les grandir et les lier les uns aux autres par l'exaltation lucide de leur responsabilité.*[47]

As with any absolute solution to a social problem, Rivière's society brought inevitable hardship to people who failed, or contradicted his ideals. For the pilot Fabien this meant death. But for Rivière, like Saint-Exupéry, death is not tragic. It is regrettable, never for one moment does he deny this or underestimate its importance – it is a setback in the common struggle, but it must not be over emphasized.

Similarly other people are adversely affected by Rivière's discipline. Roblet, the employee with a long record of

---

[45] p. 121.
[46] p. 135.
[47] Chevrier, p. 50.

irreproachable service is dismissed because of one mistake. Robineau, the inspector, is denied the right to enjoy the comradeship with the pilots that he would like because of his superior position. The pilot's wife is separated sorrowfully from her husband before each flight.

Finally there is the shattering of a world which must be completely alien to Rivière's world of action, though he recognizes the importance of those who believe in it. This world is now typified by Simone Fabien. Before it was shattered by Fabien's death it had been a world of peace and happiness, the world of simple, human joys rather than superhuman satisfactions.

> *Mais sa vérité était si forte que les regards fugitifs remontaient à la dérobée, inlassablement, la lire dans son visage. Cette femme était très belle. Elle révélait à quelle matière auguste on touche sans le savoir, en agissant.... Elle révélait quelle paix, sans savoir, on peut détruire.*[48]

But of course none of these setbacks, no mundane consideration, can thwart Rivière in his determination to succeed, in his will to preserve his thriving community. Thus we see that the last chapter is an optimistic one:

> *La défaite qu'a subie Rivière est peut-être un engagement qui rapproche la vraie victoire.*[49]

The final victory if there is such a thing as a final victory, is perhaps one step nearer and Rivière is still at the helm, the hero responsible for the fullness of his pilot's lives:

> *Rivière-le-Grand, Rivière-le-Victorieux, qui porte sa lourde victoire.*[50]

---

[48] p. 128.
[49] p. 136.
[50] p. 136.

CHAPTER THREE
Terre des Hommes : THE FIRST UNIVERSAL SOLUTION

In the next work, *Terre des Hommes* published in 1939, there is no Rivière. Chevrier tells us that Saint-Exupéry is now only interested in the individual in so far as he can draw universal conclusions from his behaviour.

> *Il ne s'intéresse au singulier que pour en tirer des constantes*[51]

He goes on to say that Saint-Exupéry is interested in the universal values of civilization that one can see through the individual.

It may be possible that Chevrier underestimates the importance of the individual for Saint-Exupéry. It is certain, however that in *Terre des Hommes* he seems to be turning his attention away from the specific to the general. Rivière was, as it were, the "god" of his limited universe. There is now no guide or enlightened despot. This is the *Terre des Hommes*, the world covered with men going about their different ways, discovering their own values in a somewhat arbitrary and chaotic manner. And so Saint-Exupéry's description of the world has an arbitrary appearance about it. There are few apparent connections between one section and another. As in the world itself there is no apparent order. Nevertheless in the last section he tries to draw together his descriptive studies and find a universal pattern for human activities.

Whereas in *Vol de Nuit* it was only the hero who could find a transcendental meaning to existence, in *Terre des Hommes* it seems to be understood throughout that every man can find

---
[51] Chevrier, p. 56.

such a meaning, a meaning which is precise and definite and obeys absolute principles. We have the impression throughout the work that the author knows these principles, but is keeping them from us until "the day of judgment" when he will reveal them to us.

The nearer we get to this "day of judgment" the more the author indulges in this practice. The author, we feel, is about to reveal to his reader his considered opinion as to the real meaning behind human enterprises.

La vérité pour l'homme, c'est ce qui fait de lui un homme[52]

This we may think is leading to a revelation of the exact nature of his truth. It may well be, but before the revelation we are told of a long list of half-truths. We are given illustrations of how people with conflicting ideals are given to experiencing the same edifying sensations.

One of these illustrations[53] is taken from the Spanish Civil War. He says that for the man who has felt the awakening of the "unknown" in him by means of the discipline, sacrifice and comradeship binding him to his fellow anarchists will recognize for ever *la vérité des anarchistes*. On the other side the man who has on one occasion fought to protect a convent of nuns praying to God on their knees will recognise the truth of the Church.

But this truth is not as the examples above suggest, to be found only in a sense of fraternity. The author shows that it can be obtained through conduct which is upright and dignified,[54] through work which has a given meaning for the worker,[55]

---

[52] p. 253.
[53] p. 252.
[54] p. 253.
[55] p. 254.

through the passing on of life from one generation to another.[56] Indeed, in the case of fraternity found through warfare, its value is questionable for Saint-Exupéry.[57] Where among these assorted ideas are we to find the truth which the author has concealed from us? It is revealed to us in the last but one chapter of the book.

Here it says that man must be conscious of his role in furthering the natural progress of the human race:[58]

> *Ce que nous sentons quand nous avons faim, de cette faim…qui poussa Mermoz vers l'Atlantique Sud…c'est que la genèse n'est point achevée et qu'il nous faut prendre conscience de nous-mêmes et de l'univers. Il nous faut dans la nuit lancer des passerelles.*

An action to fulfil its objectives must have a sense beyond its immediate material implications. When Mermoz crossed over to the Chilean side of the Andes the importance was not in the fact that he had managed to carry a merchant's letter more quickly than it would otherwise have travelled, but in the fact that in doing so he had furthered human progress. He was a pioneer. Still it is the pioneer who is most important for Saint-Exupéry. After him other people can do the same thing and human achievement has been widened still more.

In this notion there is essentially a return to the two themes developed in *Courrier Sud* and *Vol de Nuit*. We are presented here with the synthesis. For there are essentially two valid ways in which a man can attain this goal of being conscious of his role in the furthering of human progress. There is the path of

---

[56] p. 257–258.
[57] p. 255–256.
[58] This, I feel, is rather more precise than the notion which Luc Estang calls "responsibility".

Geneviève and there is the path of Rivière. The former, rejected in *Vol de Nuit* in favour of the latter, is thus reinstated to its former position and indeed glorified in it, without doing so at the expense of the solution which displaced it.

Now, for Saint-Exupéry, the two values have the same status, even though he may have an unexpressed preference for one of them. The *lignée paysanne* as he calls it comes into the forefront in the section entitled *Les Hommes*. These people, we might say, are the salt of the earth. They are the people who for generation upon generation have carried the burden of human progress upon their shoulders. This progress has been not only material, but moral and social:

> *La mère n'avait point seulement transmis la vie : elle avait à ses fils, enseigné un langage, elle leur avait confié le bagage si lentement accumulé au cours des siècles, le patrimoine spirituel qu'elle avait elle-même reçu en dépôt, ce petit lot de traditions, de concepts et de mythes qui constitue toute la différence qui sépare Newton ou Shakespeare de la brute des caverne.*[59]

Somewhere along the line it would seem that progress, considerable progress, has been made. Yet it would seem fair to assume that no one individual ever made a gigantic stride, a huge leap forward similar to those taken by Mermoz. Thus each member of this *lignée paysanne* can be accredited with both preserving the progress made in the past and making a small but unmistakable step along the path of human progress. It is also very important to be conscious of this role. To act blindly seems to jar Saint-Exupéry's sensitivity, so that without stating it, the action would be absurd. On the contrary the most humble of

---

[59] p. 258.

men, a simple shepherd, can give a metaphysical justification for his *métier* if he is conscious of the social importance of the role.

> *Et ainsi jusqu'au simple berger. Car celui-là qui veille modestement quelques moutons sous les étoiles, s'il prend conscience de son rôle se découvre plus qu'un serviteur. Il est une sentinelle. Et chaque sentinelle est responsable de tout l'empire.*[60]

The hero of course is not excluded from this scheme of the world, but is given what may be considered to be a privileged position in it. The heroes of *Terre des Hommes* are real men, contemporaries and friends of the author, and indeed the author himself. There is perhaps an understandable tendency on the part of the author to be more realistic, less poetic than he had been in his fictional works. The notions expressed are however very similar.

The hero, like the peasant but to a greater extent, is conscious of his role in furthering human progress and also of the importance of maintaining civilisation at the high level it has attained. The hero is not making a small step in the name of human progress, but a huge leap forward, or, in the case of Mermoz, a whole series of leaps forward. Guillaumet, the seemingly unsuccessful hero, is no less conscious of his role in preserving those human values which man has come to cherish over the centuries.

> *Ce que j'ai fait,…jamais aucune bête ne l'aurait fait.*[61]

Indeed in his apparent failure Guillaumet not only preserves established human values by acting on behalf of his wife's social well-being, but he also achieves what might be called "moral" progress. His action shows man's latent moral and

---

[60] p. 256.
[61] p. 165.

physical courage pushed to its extreme limits: just as Mermoz had contributed to human progress on a material level, so Guillaumet has contributed to it on a moral level.

Thus as in *Vol de Nuit* by transcending the normal bounds of human activity, the heroes of *Terre des Hommes* achieve a similar sense of eternity. Even the glimpse at eternity through pantheistic wonderment remains present when we see the narrator imagining himself as part of the eternal universe, as he happens to land on a plateau in the desert, untouched since creation.[62]

And in the same way as he sees the world at its creation as he approaches middle-age he begins to look for a solution to the problem of old-age. With his new lucidity the answer seems to come quite easily to Saint-Exupéry. For when we become conscious of our role and have set about fulfilling it successfully we can enjoy the fullest of all human joys. We have a new ideal: beyond human activity lies peace, the final peace which will be ours after all our difficulties have been faced and overcome:

> *Alors seulement nous pourrons vivre en paix et mourir en paix, car ce qui donne un sens à la vie donne un sens à la mort.*[63]

This is essentially the same for the hero and the peasant. For the peasant the struggle is long and often hazardous; for the hero the struggle is comparatively short, but always exacting and hazardous. In each case, after the struggle, in old age or in death, man can enjoy the peace to which he is entitled. After the struggles Christian principles are now allowed to replace the Nietzschean tension previously necessary. Saint-Exupéry, it seems, can permit his heroes, at last, to exist in what Sartre would term as "bad faith".

---

[62] p. 174–176.
[63] p. 256.

It would be difficult to imagine any moralist basing his code of existence upon a few unadorned metaphysical principles. It would therefore be inappropriate to leave the impression that *Terre des Hommes* is a work dealing with men striving relentlessly towards a distant and absolute goal. The choice of this goal is important, as we have already seen. But when it has been chosen it brings in its wake certain human pleasures which it would be wrong to ignore, these we can group together for the sake of convenience under the title "Fraternity".

Fraternity, implicit as a natural tendency in the earlier works of Saint-Exupéry remains to a certain extent intuitive, but it's nature at least is explained in *Terre des Hommes*. The author has shown by numerous descriptions how people, when they are working together towards the same aims, feel a natural affinity, even though these aims may be execrable in moral terms. He gives the example of modern warfare. He mentions the joy of comradeship in warfare and intimates here and elsewhere that on both sides soldiers will find the same pleasures. It follows that, from a universal view-point, one or both of the ideals must be wrong. Yet he remarks that the soldiers will have achieved a limited part of their aim for eternity.

> *Ils auront trouvé ce qu'ils cherchent, le goût de l'universel. Mais du pain qui leur est offert, ils vont mourir.*[64]

When man realizes, as Saint-Exupéry realizes at the end of this chapter,[65] the real meaning of existence, it is obvious that the original intuitive tendencies will remain and will be fortified by strength and conviction in the ultimate goal.

It is now that we see the full strength of this sense of fraternity. Fraternity, or human comradeship, is the cement

---

[64] p. 255.
[65] VIII. 3.

which binds men together, which gives the fullness of their existence, which gives them a sense of belonging to the Universe. They strive not as individuals – for as individuals, like Bark the Moorish slave,[66] they are lost without the full weight of human relationships – but as a collective body in sympathy with one another. They work towards the common goal, which if right they are bound to attain:

> *Liés à nos frères par un but commun et qui se situe en dehors de nous, alors seulement nous respirons et l'expérience nous montre qu'aimer ce n'est point nous regarder l'un l'autre mais regarder ensemble dans la même direction. Il n'est de camarades que s'ils s'unissent dans le même sommet en quoi ils se retrouvent.*[67]

---

[66] Part VI Ch.6, pp.199–208.
[67] p. 252.

CHAPTER FOUR
Pilote de Guerre : THE SHATTERING OF AN IDEAL AND THE BIRTH OF A PERMANENT ONE

It is with this solution in mind, with the additional emphasis on the importance of fraternity and harmonious human relationships that Saint-Exupéry writes his next work, *Pilote de Guerre*. The three years which have elapsed since the publication of *Terre des Hommes* have however seen a complete change in the order of the world. It is now 1942 and the world is at war.

Pilote de Guerre, though far from being a novel, has a more harmonious structure than *Terre des Hommes*. Briefly it consists of a series of ethical and metaphysical reflections grouped around the author's own near-suicide mission to fly over Arras in May 1940. The action of the story brings the author face to face with the problem of "the absurd". He has one chance in three of returning alive from his mission. The photographs they are to take will be useless since France is already virtually defeated. Finally even if he does return with the photographs he may have difficulty in finding his group which is constantly on the move. The author then flies over France, the symbol of civilisation, in chaos, to meet a useless death against which he can have no defence. Only good fortune can bring him and his two comrades back safely to their quarters:

> *Il n'est rien à décider. Ça regarde Dieu exclusivement.*[68]

In the face of death the mature reflecting author of *Terre des Hommes* finds the values he had cherished, strangely lacking in substance. In the words of Luc Estang:

> *L'absurdité qu'analysait Saint-Exupéry au moment du vol d'Arras se traduisait par une 'vérité en morceaux'.*[69]

---

[68] p. 289.
[69] Luc Estang p. 125.

Even in his presentation of the old conception of human values there is a slight change of emphasis. The present truth becomes more important than the eternal truth. The distinction between the hero and the peasant virtually disappears. The author indeed is almost ashamed of being a hero. Human comradeship, a subordinate value elsewhere, is portrayed as the most important of all values. At the height of his anguish[70], expecting to be shot down in the next few seconds, Saint-Exupéry finds that human love is the most important thing in life.

> *Il faut...il faut...j'aimerais cependant être payé à temps. J'aimerais avoir droit à l'amour. J'aimerais reconnaître pour qui je meurs...*

The change of emphasis is important. Rivière, almost certainly would have said *pour quoi je meurs*. Unmistakably in his crumbling universe, Saint-Exupéry has turned his attention to humanity as a solution to his problems.

Nor is it man as an individual that is important. Bernis the outsider figure has no place in the world of 1942. Man has his value in a community. Cut off from that community he is worthless:

> *L'homme n'est qu'un nœud de relations et voilà que mes liens ne valent plus grand chose*[71]

As in all the works of Saint-Exupéry we find once more the two themes of the simple world of human relationships and of the pilot freed from the bounds of a limited existence. As in *Terre des Hommes* these elements are no longer conflicting but there is still a slight difference: though both are dependent upon the *nœud de relations* both are vitally afflicted if the thread of this "knot" is broken.

---

[70] Ch.7, p. 288.
[71] Ch.14, p. 311.

For the peasant this "knot" can be compared to a cartwheel whose driving force is in the hub which symbolizes for us the village community. The outer rim of the wheel is made up of the individual peasants bound to each other and bound to the community as a whole by the stout sense of belonging which the thick wooden spokes convey to us. In this community there is no place for the outsider. The narrowness of its limits is counterbalanced by the breadth and density of the bonds which weld them together. Each member of the community is responsible for the well-being of the others, just as each member is dependent upon the others for his own well-being. If one member of the community frees himself from these bonds the community no longer exists. Thus during the general evacuation before the German invasion, Saint-Exupéry and his friend Dutertre persuade the inhabitants of the village, where they are living, that they would be well advised to stay put rather than flee before the enemy. They are all agreed but they are forced to leave:

> ...*le boulanger est parti. Qui fera le pain ? Le village est déjà détraqué. Il a crevé ici ou là. Tout coulera par le même trou. C'est sans espoir.*[72]

The pilot's "knot" is much less symmetrical. It is more like loose strands of wool all jumbled up together. It has no limits except the ends of the earth. Some of his friends know each other, some are unknown to the others. The common bond is the pilot, the man in the centre of this *nœud de relations*. Without his bonds of friendship the man in the centre ceases to exist. As each bond is destroyed the man loses a part of his personality. On the other hand while the bond exists the man is shaped,

---

[72] p. 320.

replenished and edified by his friends. The thicker his bonds and the more numerous his friends the fuller is his life.

These are the real things which Saint-Exupéry cherishes and these are the things that will be lost if he dies. But as he reflects on his flight he realizes that some of the things at least can be salvaged. Indeed, in his own life, he finds as he emerges from behind the enemy lines, his bonds of friendship have been intensified. Whereas before he felt unworthy of his friends he was now sure that he belonged to them and they belonged to him.

Life at a personal level has a meaning – intrinsic if not transcendental. He has, like his comrade, Hochedé, found the right to exist in a community. What is now most important for the individual is to be accepted as an integral and necessary part of the community. To be accepted one must have filled the requirements, all the requirements of that community. Thus the hero, or the author, can be accepted at the peasant's table if he accepts the invitation with humility, as a participant, not as an onlooker:

> *Ce livre eût pu me donner l'apparence d'un témoin abstrait. Et cependant je ne faisais figure, malgré lui, ni d'intellectuel, ni de témoin. J'étais des leurs.*[73]

Even more important for the pilot is the fact that he can now participate to the full in the real comradeship of the Group 2/33. The fraternity of this group is deep and sincere. Right of entry into this fraternity is gained by the man who has suffered the same trials as the other pilots.

> *Je ne suis pas le citadin qui joue, en vacances, au paysan. J'ai été chercher, une fois de plus, la preuve de ma bonne foi sur Arras. J'ai*

---

[73] p. 354.

> *engagé ma chair dans l'aventure. Toute ma chair. Et je l'ai engagée perdante. J'ai donné tout ce que j'ai pu à ces règles du jeu. Pour qu'elles soient autre chose que des règles du jeu. J'ai acquis le droit de me sentir penaud, bientôt, quand le Commandant n'interrogera. C'est-à-dire de participer. D'être lié.*[74]

The ultimate sense of belonging has only been attained by a pilot called Hochedé. He is a hero in the true sense of the word. He is a man who is a natural volunteer, a natural participant:

> *Hochedé est volontaire naturellement. Il est cette guerre. C'est si naturel que, s'il s'agit d'un équipage à sacrifier, le commandant pense aussitôt à Hochedé.*[75]

Now after his mission Saint-Exupéry is more *pétri de liens* than he was before. The reason for Hochedé's full belonging to the community is that he is *pétri de liens*. He is directly attached to things that exist, things for which he will fight to the last:

> *Il luttera pour son chronomètre. Son chronomètre existe. Et il mourra pour son pays. Son pays existe. Hochedé existe, qui est lié à eux. Il est pétri de tous ses liens avec le monde.*[76]

Similarly, as we noted above, if one of these bonds of friendship is destroyed, part of the man himself is destroyed. Thus when Guillaumet is killed, there is a part of the author that dies at the same time:

> *Je me sens un peu mort en lui. J'ai fait de Guillaumet un des compagnons de mon silence. Je suis de Guillaumet.*[77]

Thus, Saint-Exupéry has proved himself strong enough to withstand the anguish caused by the apparent absurdity of

---

[74] p. 355.
[75] p. 356.
[76] p. 357.
[77] p. 352.

warfare. His immediate life is strengthened. He can look forward to a fuller existence because of the sacrifice he was asked to make. This is not true of France as a whole. Civilisation, as it had been understood in France, has been destroyed by the advancing German army. Hundreds of peasant communities had similarly been destroyed. For ever optimistic, Saint-Exupéry is convinced that there is some reason for the hopeless pitting of forty million French peasants against eighty million German industrial workers. Using a Cartesian method of analysis he sets about resolving his problem.

He analyses what has happened to the values that have been so dear to the civilized French man. By analysing an army in disorderly retreat and comparing it with the victorious army, he tries to find out what happened to the morale of the defeated army, the defeated army which symbolizes his broken ideals. He hopes by this method to find a universal justification for this defeat which at the moment appears absurd.

He finds that victory unites the army, defeat disintegrates it. Each defeated Frenchman contains in himself the properties of France, the defeated nation, and of civilisation in ruins:

> *Si les fuyards ne pleurent pas sur la France qui croule, c'est parce qu'ils sont vaincus. C'est parce que la France est défaite non autour d'eux mais en eux-mêmes. Pleurer sur la France serait déjà être vainqueur.*[78]

A comparison could be made between France and a cannon ball. While it is whole it has potential force. Should it disintegrate into atoms by some scientific process, each of the atoms still retains the properties of the cannon ball, but, without the power to unite with others it is useless.

---

[78] p. 330.

The conclusion we would draw is that France's sacrifice has been absurd. France has been destroyed. Individual personalities have been destroyed. Comradeship has been destroyed. Life for these men no longer has any meaning.

Saint-Exupéry thinks differently. Out of the ruins will grow a new, virile civilisation. As in his personal world participation in this civilisation can only be full if accompanied by the total sacrifice of each individual to that civilisation. Forty million Frenchmen have made that sacrifice, the rest of the world must benefit from it:

> *La France a joué son rôle. Il consistait pour elle à se proposer à l'écrasement, puisque le monde arbitrait sans collaborer ni combattre, et à se voir ensevelir pour un temps dans le silence. Quand on donne l'assaut il est nécessairement des hommes en tête. Ceux-là meurent presque toujours. Mais il faut pour que l'assaut soit que les premiers meurent.*[79]

The French have made the supreme sacrifice. They have served as an example to the world. The world will follow their example. From their sacrifice will be born the hopes of a new civilisation.

The value of human life consists in this total sacrifice which must be active and not indifferent, of oneself to the body of which one would be a part. Saint-Exupéry compares this sacrifice to someone working on an estate:

> *Celui-là seul comprendra ce qu'est un domaine, qui lui aura sacrifié une part de soi, qui aura lutté pour le sauver, et peiné pour l'embellir. Alors lui viendra l'amour du domaine. Un domaine n'est pas la somme des intérêts, là est l'erreur. Il est la somme des dons.*[80]

---

[79] p. 332.
[80] p. 377.

It is upon this idea of participation through sacrifice that the whole code of human behaviour that we find in the last third of *Pilote de Guerre* is constructed.

Saint-Exupéry at last has found a universal solution to the meaning of human existence. The individual Frenchman is part of France which is part of Humanity (we note the Capital "H"). Saint-Exupéry calls this concept *l'Homme*. France has sacrificed her individuals to create the hope which will provide the adhesive substance necessary to unite her desperate individuals into this new super-comradeship called Humanity. Humanity is the unification through sacrifice of all men for their mutual benefit and enrichment:

> *Ma civilisation repose sur le culte de l'Homme au travers des individus. Elle a cherché des siècles durant, à montrer l'Homme, comme elle eût enseigné à distinguer une cathédrale à travers des pierres. Elle a prêché cet Homme qui dominait l'individu… Car l'Homme de ma civilisation ne se définit pas à partir des hommes. Ce sont les hommes qui se définissent par lui. Il est en lui, comme en tout être, quelque chose que n'expliquent pas les matériaux qui le composent. Une cathédrale est bien autre chose qu'une somme de pierres. Elle est géométrie et architecture. Ce ne sont pas les pierres qui la définissent, c'est elle qui enrichit les pierres de sa propre signification …*[81]

There is no need then to seek any further for a transcendental value for life. This value is to be found in Humanity. Man by sacrificing his personal interests to that cause will be wholeheartedly accepted by the cause and will be improved and embellished by it. The new question which one must inevitably

---

[81] p. 372.

ask oneself is: what would be the position of the individual in this society which appears so similar to the near-totalitarian society of Rivière?

Saint-Exupéry rejects totalitarianism:

> *Je-combattrai quiconque prétendra asservir à un individu --- comme à une masse d'individus – la liberté de l'Homme*[82]

The new civilisation will be founded on individual liberty:

> Or *ma civilisation a cherché à fonder les relations humaines sur le culte de l'Homme au-delà de l'individu, afin que le comportement de chacun vis-à-vis de soi-même ou d'autrui ne soit plus conformisme aveugle aux usages de la termitière mais libre exercice d'amour.*[83]

His civilisation, he admits, is based on Christian ethics. He takes seven Christian virtues and translates them into virtues of his civilisation. The virtues are: Liberty, Equality, Respect for one's fellow men, Fraternity, Charity, Self-respect and Responsibility.

It seems that Fraternity and Responsibility have been put on the same level as a host of other virtues. This is not quite true. There is an essential rule of conduct which the author proposes for himself upon which the survival of the society depends. This rule is based upon solidarity with those belonging to the same body or community as oneself. If a man belongs to a family, he must not renounce that family. If he cannot defend a miscreant, the best he can do is to observe silence on the matter. For each person is responsible for the moral well-being of the community to which he belongs. It is his duty to rise up inside that community and inspire it along the right path. Hochedé typifies this attitude:

---

[82] p. 383.
[83] p. 373.

> *Hochedé ne rejette pas la défaite sur d'autres que lui. Il se dit : « moi, Hochedé, moi de France j'ai été faible. La France de Hochedé a été faible. J'ai été faible en elle et elle faible en moi ».*[84]

This does not mean, as one might be led to believe, that Saint-Exupéry is advocating social conformism. He is advocating that the individual should fight for a revival of those basically Christian principles which would defeat the mediocrity that has taken its roots in modern society. Man must be liberated so that he will be capable of ruling himself,[85] and of directing himself towards the desired goal.

His basic aim, like that of Rivière, is to further human achievement by allowing only the enriching human values to prevail and by suppressing mediocrity:

> *Je combattrai quiconque, prétendant que ma charité honore la médiocrité, reniera l'Homme et ainsi emprisonnera l'individu dans une médiocrité définitive.*[86]

Human achievement, he maintains, can best be furthered by fighting for universal values against particular interests. In this way individual weaknesses will be suppressed. Only the transcendental qualities will remain. By his sacrifice to the cause of Humanity, the individual will improve that cause. That is the essence of life:

> *Je crois que le culte de l'universel exalte et noue les richesses particulières – et fonde le seul ordre véritable, lequel est celui de la vie*[87]

---

[84] p. 368.
[85] p. 373.
[86] p. 383.
[87] p. 383.

CONCLUSION

Now that we have seen the development of Saint-Exupéry's thought from the early days of *Courrier Sud* to his last major completed work, it is possible by way of conclusion to examine the main themes that have been noted and to consider their development.

The development of the hero is perhaps the most interesting. The concept is born in *Courrier Sud* of an ardent need to escape from the earthbound existence, on the part of Bernis. The failure of Bernis to achieve anything but a sense of bewilderment and frustration is, paradoxically, closely related to the success of the heroes of *Vol de Nuit*. Bernis was frustrated because his action was not directed towards an ideal but was merely action for action's sake. This theme is constant. Later on Saint-Exupéry is to condemn the toreador on the same grounds. The hero's action has a meaning only in so far as it is directed towards a definite goal, be it a limited one as in *Vol de Nuit*, or part of a universal pattern as in *Terre des Hommes* and *Pilote de Guerre*.

The hero of *Vol de Nuit* is almost a pure hero. He thrusts away the world of simple happiness, even though it has some attraction for him. Rivière's world is an absolute world, there is no time for human love. This conception is purely Nietzschean: for Rivière

> *it is necessary to kill the man so that the superman may live.*

From *Terre des Hommes* onwards the hero ceases to be apart from the common throng. The new note is struck: everyone becomes a hero. There are no longer two absolute poles apart but a graded hierarchy of heroic attributes from those of the simple shepherd to those of the pilot-adventurer. The latter is still at the top of the hierarchy, but we feel his autonomy diminishing. By *Pilote de Guerre* it has almost disappeared. The important thing is that Humanity as a whole should strive through individual upsurges to self-surpassment. The hero no longer seeks to show his superiority over the common throng. His value is measured in terms of the strength of his ties with his fellow men and the strength he adds to the common effort.

It is indeed the theme of Fraternity which takes over the role of the hero concept. As the hero diminishes in stature, Fraternity grows in importance. There is little room for Fraternity in *Courrier Sud*, Bernis is at his happiest when alone in the aeroplane; he believes there is something more important than human love of any kind. In *Vol de Nuit* Fraternity is only permitted among equals. The need is already felt strongly and urgently by Robineau, but he his reprimanded for it. He is not in a position to fraternize with the pilots whom he has under his control. In *Terre des Hommes* and *Pilote de Guerre* it blossoms out to its full proportions. It becomes the joy that makes life worth living, indeed the prime need of man if he is to achieve the goals he has set himself.

The world of simple human relationships undergoes a similar fate. Given as the key to all human activity in *Courrier Sud* it is rejected as incompatible with the heroic goals which man was made to aim for. This rejection is reiterated in *Vol de Nuit*. In *Terre des Hommes* it becomes identified with the simple peasant community and the *lignée paysanne*, the handing down of the family traditions from one generation to another. Its value has been re-established. Indeed, it is by reflection upon one such family that the author arrives at the notion of human progress as the new goal at which to aim. It is the breaking up of the small village community during the war that Saint-Exupéry regrets the most. It is for its preservation that he is fighting. His new personal solution to the problem of existence is modelled on this *nœud de relations* to which he has come to attach so much importance.

All these themes have a common denominator. The quest is for eternity. Geneviève finds a sort of eternity and so do the heroes of *Vol de Nuit.* Their eternity is different and each kind is incomprehensible to the other. It is largely the eternity found by Geneviève that is accepted as the true basis for true eternity: the identification of the individual with a cause that goes beyond the bounds of human mortality. But the hero's conception of eternity is not forgotten, for it is as a development of this that Saint-Exupéry forms the idea that the individual must be conscious of his role in the evolution that is taking place. That is the essential theme of *Terre des Hommes* and *Pilote de Guerre.*

Thus the conflict which was suggested in the Introduction as one of the seeds of Saint-Exupéry's works, has been resolved. The author has found a meaning to human existence which he can accept without conflict. A meaning which satisfies his needs and fulfils all ideals.

This final solution to the problem of human existence has one basic fault. If this society is to be created, how can the author expect men with their own ideas and interests to submit themselves to his demands? Even he admits that he has forgotten these principles at the beginning of his flight over Arras:

> *Mais peu à peu j'ai oublié ma vérité.*[88]

---

[88] p. 372.

Thus from the basically realistic solution of *Terre des Hommes*, Saint-Exupéry has become very much an idealist, though it must be admitted that his ideals had considerable propaganda value in the United States when *Pilote de Guerre* was first published there as *Flight to Arras*.

The unfinished work *Citadelle* provides a logical conclusion to Saint-Exupéry's thought. Just as the ideal sought for in *Courrier Sud* is realized by the firm discipline imposed by Rivière on the pilots in *Vol de Nuit,* so the ideal of *Pilote de Guerre* finds its expression in the enlightened despotism of the desert chieftain. The meaning of existence remains the same for the individual: self-surpassment becoming once more the main object. The only problem which is given a vitally different aspect is one which we have not considered in detail, the problem of individual liberty. Thus the pilot, who fought against totalitarianism, is seen a few years later advocating despotism as the only feasible solution.

It is an admission of defeat on the part of the author. He realizes that his own ideals, if not contrary to human nature in general, are at least contrary to current trends. His last correspondence shows his personal anguish before the growth of *impersonalisme* and pseudo-"American" values. The values which he had set out in his works were trodden underfoot. His final notes are despairing. In his letter, *Lettre au General X*, we read the following words:

> *Ça m'est bien égal d'être tué en guerre. De ce que j'ai aimé, que restera-t-il ? Autant que des êtres, je parle des coutumes, les intonations irremplaçables, d'une certaine lumière spirituelle.*[89]

---

[89] Quoted by Chevrier p.188.

It is difficult to see how Saint-Exupéry could have carried any further his message of hope. He was sure there was a meaning to existence: he set out to find it and he evolved his solution. But when he faced up to reality Saint-Exupéry was doomed to despair, for his solution was almost "idealistic": it was a glimpse of the essence of life. Human values on the other hand had become more materialistic, more superficial, according to his standards. The trend towards mass-culture, or rather mass-entertainment, shocked him because of the debasement of "spiritual" and artistic values that followed in their wake. These trends have provided a constant butt for the criticism of post-war artists. Could Saint-Exupéry have forced himself to make a new start and join the bandwagon of social satire, as his last letters suggest that he was about to do? Or, would he, as the still small voice, have continued to advocate his own solution carefully evolved through the years of his manhood?

BIBLIOGRAPHICAL NOTE

Reference to the works of Antoine Saint-Exupéry are taken from the *Pléiade* edition of his works published by *Gallimard (nrf)* July 1959. These references are simply indicated by page numbers. Other references are to the following editions:

Pierre-Henri Simon : *L'Homme en Procès* (La Baconnière, Neuchâtel, 1950).

Pierre Chevrier : *Saint-Exupéry* (Bibliothèque Idéale, Gallimard, 1958).

Luc Estang : *Saint-Exupéry par lui-même* (Ecrivains de Toujours, Editions du Seuil, 1959).

André Malraux : *Les Conquérants* (Livre de Poche).

Acknowledgements

I would like to thank Jon first of all for persuading me to write this book and then for all his work in preparing it for publication.

I would also like to thank Jennifer for her painstaking work in retyping the faded typescript of my thesis.

www.ingramcontent.com/pod-product-compliance
Lightning Source LLC
Chambersburg PA
CBHW071201070526
44584CB00019B/2874